JACKIE VANN

D1468568

THE PAPER BAG

How to Extract Hope from Hopelessness

The Paper Bag: How to Extract Hope from Hopelessness
By Jackie Vann

ISBN-13: 978-1478354833
ISBN-10: 1478354836

Contact Jackie Vann at vannjackie1@gmail.com

Cover design by Yvonne Parks at www.pearcreative.ca
Internal design by David Sluka at www.hitthemarkpublishing.com

Printed in the United States of America

Dedication

*To my sister and brother-in-law, Sandra and Jack.
You became my "Aarons" and held me together when I
was imploding. Your loving kindness, steadfast words
of encouragement at every turn, and your sacrificial
financial support I can never repay!*

Acknowledgements

THANK YOU to my sister Lynda, who asked when I first began to write the book if it would be OK if she corrected some of the phrasing, and ended up sticking it out to its completion. She was able to capture my deepest anguish and put wings to my words.

Thank you to Roger and my children, whose buffeting enabled me to become the person I am today.

Thank you to Joyce Meyer, whose ministry helped me to have a deeper awareness of God's unconditional love and acceptance of me.

Thank you David Sluka for taking on this adventure with me and making this book a reality.

Most importantly, I thank God who made all this possible by being my constant companion and guiding my footsteps as I walked through treacherous dark valleys and desert experiences. He put a burden upon my heart to write all this down for the sole purpose of ministering hope to those of you who have had similar tragedies and feel there is no hope. To those readers who were blessed not to have had to experience this type of upheaval, this story might make you all the more thankful. If there is one thing I want readers to learn from *The Paper Bag*, it is that there is always **hope** no matter what you're facing in life. If you're convinced you've lost "it," you haven't; it's probably just temporarily derailed or misplaced, and He will help you find it again.

Contents

Preface

THERE ARE SOME TRAGEDIES that happen in everyone's life at one time or another that are just too overwhelming for the human heart to endure. Just when you think things couldn't possibly get any worse, they do. Going from a carefully-planned future to most of the time feeling mentally fragmented and physically ill, and longing for God to remove you from your grotesque nightmare, was never in the cards. Unfortunately, we don't get a do-over or a practice run as we try to navigate through what life throws our way and, often times, our very core and spiritual fiber is stretched and challenged to the breaking point, while we struggle to try to make sense out of it all.

When we stand at those crossroads, we can do one of two things: give in to the overbearing inevitability of the enormous mountain ahead, or dig down deep, find our spiritual compass, and hang on for dear life, confident that when we emerge from our unsolicited nightmare, we will feel empowered and undefeatable. Life somehow takes on a whole new meaning as the old adage "it'll either make you or break you" becomes reality on a day-by-day and sometimes moment-by-moment basis.

As our faith becomes more definitive, God will seem close yet far at the same time. I learned quickly that living faith is altogether different than talking about it. Although we may never be able to fully understand why things happen to us, it is important to believe and trust God, for the scripture says, "All things work together for good to those who love Him and are called according to His purpose". No matter what disaster penetrates our world, we can confidently set our faces toward Him and know that He will walk with us. And after all is said and done, as long as we choose to hold onto our faith through the sorrow, confusion, and pain, we will reap the greater reward. Jesus said, "If we endure to the end, we will be saved."

Introduction

WHILE VACUUMING THE SUN PORCH one day, I was on the last lap, approaching the mammoth bookcase, which flanked the side wall. Out of the corner of my eye, I caught a glimpse of something sticking out from behind the cabinet. What is that? I thought maybe a piece of paper or bag must have slipped down there, so I bent over and slowly pulled it from its safely-hidden spot. I peered inside and in a split second, my world unraveled and life as I knew it would never be the same again. During the next number of years, I found myself standing at life's crossroads that presented me with the choice to give up, break under the pressure and walk away from my faith in God, or face the looming giant and battle head on *with* Him one day at a time and one battle at a time. I questioned my faith, my ability, and God's ability to get me through this complete devastation as my foundation was rocked to the core.

The contents inside "the paper bag" would forever change my life and set in motion a cyclonic storm that wreaked havoc, fear, devastation, and annihilation of not only my life, but that of my children's also. The bag contained my past, my present, and my future. It obliterated our security and flung us into a life we didn't ask for and were unprepared to face. It caused unbelievable hardship and pain, and had no regard for the massive destruction it would inflict upon each one of us. The chaos would follow us relentlessly for years to come. Oh God, help me...

1

my Story

I was born into a middle-class Christian home, the third of four girls. Like all men, my father wished for a son. Each time the nurse would come out of the operating room and announce, "It's a girl," I picture my dad being disappointed for a split second, but then becoming like a proud peacock. In those days, babies were treated like a fine piece of china and handled with kid gloves for fear of breaking them. Germs were a threat and precaution was taken to a new level. The day we were brought home from the hospital, with each precious daughter, he would hover over us, keeping visitors and siblings at arm's length so as not to contaminate us. He even made visitors put on face masks for the first ten or so days of our lives. After the fourth announcement, "It's a girl," he decided to give up trying to have a son. Nevertheless, he doted over "his girls" when we were little, and accepted his destiny of being the only male in the household which included a female dog and birds.

Dad was the heating inspector for the city of St. Louis Park and mom was a homemaker, seamstress, painter, artist, and wonderful cook. We felt well cared for and loved as we burst through the door after school and smelled the cinnamon rolls just coming out of the oven. Dad cooked one thing that he claimed was his specialty—chow mein; he boasted that it was his "own" perfected recipe. If I remember correctly, I don't think we shared his enthusiasm! Lucky for us, he only made it once a year or so. Mom and dad did a lot of canning back then; applesauce, bing cherries, peaches, pears, sauerkraut, sweet corn, and tomatoes. The jars were lovingly placed in a small pantry under the steps in the basement and became our food stash for the winter months. Ours was a simple life during those growing up years and looking back on them now brings back good kid memories.

Dad was very frugal throughout most of the year, so Christmas time was extra special when he pulled out all the stops to make sure we got a few things we had been begging for all year long. The only other time he was generous and opened up his wallet was when we would take our one week's annual vacation up in northern Minnesota at a resort called Bear Paw Lodge. I remember it being a time that we were allowed to consume junk food in abundance along with ice cream, candy, and fresh fruits. The rest of the year, treats like that were not readily accessible to us. Needless to say, we took full advantage!

Dad enjoyed woodworking, and made a coffee table and lamp when he and mom were newly married. He also made my little sister a rocking horse for Christmas one year and a giant Santa Claus that was adhered to the front of our house for all in our neighborhood to see and enjoy during the holiday season.

Mom came from a very poor background: the complete opposite of dad's. They met at my dad's cousin's house where mom did housekeeping and ironing chores. She was naturally beautiful and slimly built with a shy personality. It didn't take long, however, for them to become engaged. Her wedding dress was knee-length: black silk trimmed with a white collar. She didn't have money to buy a fancy wedding gown and ended up borrowing a dress from her best friend. She was ecstatic to marry above her class and looked forward to a better life.

Shortly after mom and dad were married, they purchased a tiny house in Crystal, Minnesota. It was so small it had an outhouse instead of an inside bathroom. They raised some chickens and grew all their own vegetables. The house became a home, and mom kept it as clean and tidy as if it were her castle. A year later, my sister Sandra was born which necessitated a move to a larger place. They found a house in St. Louis Park that was a story and a half, had 3 more bedrooms, and an inside bathroom. Dad was able to also purchase the three lots to the left and one lot to the right of our house. My sister Lynda and I were born in that house. Dad used one of the extra lots to build a basement house for mom's parents to live in. As kids, we became very close to Grandma and Grandpa Makousky! Grandma was the first one in the family to become a believer in Jesus and she worked tirelessly to try and get her family to accept Him as well.

Our mother was a phenomenal seamstress. Over the years, I remember her sewing a gorgeous formal for Miss St. Louis Park, worn at her coronation. Mom also made a reversible sailor suit for an entertainer who, half way through his act, turned it inside out and it glowed in the dark when they put black lights on him. She was also contracted to design and sew outfits for the St. Louis Park Parkettes dance troop. We could always count on something made with love by her at Christmas and were thrilled to get anything; it didn't matter that it was handmade. The rest of the year, we did with what we had unless our shoes fell apart prematurely or we ridiculously outgrew our clothes. There wasn't much extra money then but our needs were met.

My father came from a well-heeled family from Fairmont, Minnesota. His father, uncle, and grandmother were doctors/osteopaths, and his mother a socialite. He had a nanny and the finest clothes growing up. Unfortunately, both his parents passed away at relatively young age, so he was thrust out on his own and parentless at the age of twenty-one. He was left with the responsibility of his fourteen-year-old sister and made the regrettable decision to put her in a boarding school—a decision that would haunt him for years to come. They were estranged and barely knew each other as adults. I only remember her visiting us a couple of times. Her bright red lipstick was unforgettable to me. We lost track of her and with a little detective work, quite by accident, found her via Facebook in early 2010 through her daughter Kelly. We were ecstatic and shocked to discover dad's only sibling was still alive and living in Modesto, California. Unfortunately, we also discovered she was suffering from dementia and other serious ailments. She passed away later that year and is now fellowshipping with her brother in heaven where the past is forgotten.

Dad rarely talked about his life as a child growing up in the wealthy well-respected family. Over the years, our curiosity would surface and we would ask questions about his boyhood and family memories only to get much abbreviated answers indicating he wasn't willing to discuss it with us. We never understood his hesitancy. The only one he would talk about was his uncle, Flavius Josephus, who had a farm somewhere in Missouri. Every summer he was put on a train with a note pinned to his lapel containing the information about where he was going and who would be meeting him when he arrived.

After his parents passed away, he inherited a substantial estate, but with no direction or supervision, and left to his own immature devices, he quickly blew through most of it with nothing to show. After sowing his wild oats, he finally came to his senses, became frugal and hard-working, and would go on to purchase and pay for three homes during his lifetime.

He was a strict father and, as they would say, ruled the roost. Mom wasn't involved in the finances and didn't know until the day he passed away, at age sixty-eight, what provisions he had or hadn't made for her in the event of his death. She was sixty-one at the time of his death and had never paid a bill, wrote out a check, or purchased groceries. He did all that for her. She was a submissive, happy wife and mother most of the time.

In retrospect, as I look back on my upbringing, I now see that I took on the same roll in my marriage. My individuality and personality slowly became nonexistent as Roger took control. I ceased being "me" and, by becoming totally submissive, I ended up paying a huge price. I trusted without question and lost my ability to think critically. Jackie Jones became Roger's wife.

I had some health issues when I was little. I was plagued with eczema all over my body to the point that my mother had to soak gauze in a solution of some kind and wrap my arms, legs, and neck. It was torturous. Back then, the doctors gave it their best guess as to what the cause was. Now days, they do allergy testing and can pinpoint, in great detail, what the problem is. My skin was itchy, red, dry, and cracking. It was painful and restrictive for days and months on end. My physical struggle was hard on me and on the family. Wool and feathers were my enemies and I couldn't have peanut butter, eggs, chocolate, bananas, or tomato-based products. Even though I was cut off from these foods, the eczema continued with a vengeance and persisted endlessly. Winter months were the worst. During the summer, it cleared up for the most part and eventually I outgrew its effects. I also had a propensity for pneumonia, which I contracted most winters.

I know God had His hand on me even back then as I was growing up. I was a curious child, retreating into my own little world with whatever was on my mind at the time. I never needed to be entertained and was more than content to entertain myself. People used to have to speak my name often and loudly to get my attention. I vividly remember an incident that happened when I was five years old. My parents decided to pack a lunch and take the family on a picnic. It was such a beautiful, sunny day and we were all very excited. We arrived at the park and got everything unpacked and settled in our perfect spot. My two older sisters were busy doing what they do and no one was paying any attention to me. As was my nature, I wandered away from the safety of the family to explore my surroundings. I was out of sight in a split second.

I came upon what I thought was a nice sandy pond and saw a little turtle that said (in my mind), "Hi, come follow me and play." It was too tempting for a five year old to resist. It moved onto the watery, sandy surface of the pond. As I stepped off the edge to reach for it, I felt my feet sinking. I sunk down further and further until I was in up my chest. I struggled, clawed, and grabbed for the grass but as soon as I got a handful, it let loose from the dirt: roots and all. For some reason, even at five years old, I knew that God needed to make the roots stay in so I could pull myself out. I prayed that the grass within my reach would stay in and He must have heard my little prayer. I reached for the last few tufts. They held, and I was able to pull myself out. I ran back to my parents as fast as I could. Just about that time, they noticed I was missing and started to look for me. When I appeared, they could see that my clothes were wet and sandy high up on my body and began to question me as to what had happened. As the story unfolded, they became visually shaken and asked where the pond was. I showed them and that's when they discovered that it was quick sand! I remember them grabbing me, hugging me, and crying as they thanked God for sparing my life.

Also, as a child I was intrigued by fire. I don't know why, but it was mesmerizing to me. One particular day, my sister found me walking up and down the alley, in my own little world, swinging a small purse into which I had put something I had retrieved out of the burn barrel. It was still on fire and smoking. Again, God kept me safe: this time from setting my clothes on fire and severely burning myself. Needless to say, I got quite the talking to and was warned never to do anything like that again.

I was a child full of love for everything! I kissed my dolls, furniture, floor, animals, my reflection in a mirror, and any person who would come within close proximity—much to the chagrin of my two older sisters. To this day, as a grandmother, I am known by one of my grandchildren as "grandma kissy." My parents used to say, you better marry a man who enjoys lots of affection because he's going to get it whether he likes it or not!

Our family went to a church called Calvary Temple Soul's Harbor. After seeing a television program of the same name, my parents was immediately drawn to the charismatic minister, music, and message they heard, so decided to give it a try. We loved it and made it our church home, attending services every time the church doors were open. We grew up in the youth group, sang in the choirs, and made wonderful friends. We received our faith compass and foundation for serving the Lord as we sat under one of the greatest pastors of that time, Rev. Gordon K. Peterson. He preached hell, fire, and brimstone and the love of God. He told it like it was. Hundreds, if not thousands, of people gave their lives to the Lord over the years as a result of this ministry. We enjoyed the best music, teaching, and preaching. We had many outside evangelists, teachers, singing groups, and opportunities to be involved in a wonderful life-changing ministry.

During high school, I landed a job at Totino's Pizza. I worked on an assembly line topping the pizzas. It wasn't the best job, but it was a job. The only problem was that I reeked like pizza after my shift. My waist-long, thick hair, clothes, and skin absorbed the odors and when I came home, it was more than mom could stomach. She made me hang my clothes and coat out on the porch for fear of contaminating everything in the house. Then I would jump in the shower, wash my hair, and put on clean, freshly-laundered clothes. There was nothing better!

2

Attitude Adjustment

WHILE ATTENDING SOUL'S HARBOR, a man named Don Nelson found freedom from alcoholism and a past that tortured him with horrific memories of his experiences in a concentration camp during World War II. He was in the camp for a year. After the war ended and he returned home to the States, those wartime experiences haunted him and filled him with anger. This ultimately affected and sabotaged his relationships and ability to make a life for himself and his wife, Gen. He felt hopeless and helpless, unable to find peace and forgiveness. In order to dull the memories, alcohol became his drug of choice.

One Sunday, he was invited by an old friend to attend a service at Soul's Harbor and found what he had been searching for his whole life. He felt the supernatural love of Jesus flooding his soul and healing him of the pain that plagued him for so many years. He walked out of those church doors a completely different man. He began to serve the Lord with his whole heart. He joined a quartet at the church and sang and played guitar for them. His marriage and other relationships were restored and he was a grateful man, fully dedicated to the God who had saved him from himself and eternity in hell.

As time went on, he felt a distinct call of God upon his life to share the salvation message of Jesus in remote villages deep in the interior of Alaska where the people had no way to get to churches to hear about this wonderful Jesus. Many of these villages were accessible only by plane, so he decided to become a bush pilot in order to deliver the message that was burning in his heart. There he found people who were hungry to hear and embrace Don and the message of Jesus' love for them.

He had many near death experiences trying to land his little airplane on less than favorable landing strips during inhospitable weather conditions: sometimes it was grass, makeshift patches of a dirt road, or, on occasion, ice. He began to try and think of how he could reach more natives without taking such horrendous chances and possibly getting himself killed.

He had a wife and daughter and wanted to live to a ripe old age while at the same time fulfilling what God had called him to do. God gave him an idea. He had noticed during his travels to even the remotest of villages, someone always had a radio that everyone would gather around to listen to. What about putting up a radio station and beaming the gospel over radio waves? KJNP (King Jesus North Pole), an all-Christian radio station, was born. It was non-profit, staffed by volunteers, and funded through offerings. Housed in a log cabin in North Pole, Alaska, it reached into Siberia, Russia, and all over the remote territories of Alaska. That was his answer, so he went about making it happen.

I was getting a bit rebellious, as many teenagers do, and was making some poor choices. I decided to leave Minnesota and commit myself to volunteer and serve for one year on the mission field at KJNP doing whatever they needed me to do. I wanted to clear my mind and have a change of scenery. My parents agreed that it would be a good experience for me. My sister Lynda was married to Don's brother, so they felt a connection and had confidence that I would be in safe hands.

Being in Alaska at KJNP taught me a lot about commitment, submission to authority, and obedience to the Lord. It also deepened my faith. While there, I studied for and received my third-class broadcasting license, which allowed me to take on more official responsibilities. I typed out the daily FCC program schedule and helped formulate the children's program that was broadcast on Saturday mornings.

Life was simplistic at the station, and KJNP was run as a tight ship. We were expected, at all times, to be good representatives of the ministry which meant always dressing and speaking appropriately and respecting ourselves as well as each other. Rules were NOT made to be broken. Don and his wife Gen believed in modesty and strictly adhered to the scripture that said we were to "never have the appearance of evil." Because many outsiders, including people from all walks of life, would wander in and out and because it was a very rough environment, erring on the side of caution was always the best policy. The protection of the staff was Don's priority.

The bedroom I stayed in was below ground level and we could often hear and feel the rumblings of minor earthquakes. One day, as I was doing laundry in a little building on the compound, there was a major earthquake. Don always instructed us that if ever we felt an earthquake to stand in the doorway where there was more support. I glanced out and saw the ground heaving like giant waves and the tree tops passing each other as the ground was rolling. It was like viewing angry rolling waves on the ocean only without water. It was surreal to me. "Oh, my gosh," I thought, "is the radio tower gonna come down?" I knew if that happened, it would be disastrous. Fortunately, I remembered, it was located far enough behind the station (houses and other buildings on the property), that if it did collapse, it wouldn't hurt anyone or destroy too much.

It only lasted a few minutes, but seemed like an eternity. I quickly looked toward the tower and saw that only the top tier had snapped. That meant it disabled our ability to broadcast, so Don immediately called out trucks and workers to get it fixed as soon as possible. We needed to be up and running and back on air. The Eskimo and Indian people deep in the villages depended on KJNP, not only for music and religious programming but also for critical news; thus, it became a vital link to civilization for them.

KJNP was operated solely by donations and every time something like that happened, we had to trust God to bring in the money for the repairs. I quickly learned how faithful God was as I witnessed, time after time, how He provided and sustained us. I didn't realize that later on in my life, I would have to rely on Him again for my own needs.

I had many other wonderful experiences during my stay in Alaska that I will fondly remember for the rest of my life. I recall a frozen creek near the station that beckoned us to come out and play. A few of us brave souls would don our warmest gear and venture outside to ice skate in the frigid inhospitable 40-to-50-degrees-below-zero weather. We had on beautiful hand-made Alaskan parkas, and, believe it or not, they kept us so warm we got overheated and had to open them up. We also got a kick out of running into the cabin, getting small glasses of water and tossing the water high up into the air. It would immediately freeze before it hit the ground. Even though I was from Minnesota and our winters were extremely cold, I had never experienced anything like that before.

I got to witness the aurora borealis (northern lights phenomenon) from the best possible vantage point: the North Pole. The colors were spectacular and they made unforgettable eerie noises as they danced across the heavens. "How awesome God is," I thought to myself. Everything appeared larger in Alaska, most assuredly the sky.

During the short summer months, we dug up moss to cover the rooftops of any new houses, cabins, or buildings being constructed. Normal roofing products don't perform well under the extreme weather conditions we experienced, so we put sod on the roofs, which provided insulation and authenticity. Every now and then during the summer months, it had to be trimmed and it was a comical sight to see someone mowing the roof! Growing season is very short that far north, so it was important for us to plant and grow as much produce as possible to store up for the winter.

While in Alaska, during one of our regular church services, a man of God prophesied over me and said, "The man you will marry is not a Christian yet. Keep praying for him and he will give his life to the Lord Jesus. You will marry a man of God." Little did I know, at that very moment "that man" was dying in a roach-infested flop house somewhere in St. Paul, Minnesota. I began praying every day for the man who would one day become my husband. I prayed in faith believing God would answer. I then put the prophecy on the shelf and waited for its fulfillment. Later, my parents—loving and gentle people—would grimace at the thought of their daughter marrying an ex-dope addict and street bum turned preacher.

At the end of the year's stay in North Pole, it was time to for me to return to the "lower forty eights," as Don would say. When I got back, I immediately got more involved in our church and loved being at every service. I contacted an employment agency to help me acquire a job and ended up working at the JC Penney distribution office. After working all day, I would come home, change clothes, grab my Bible, and run off to a church service or prayer meeting. I wanted to be involved in the things of God more than anything and spend time with my Christian friends. My priorities had definitely changed.

One day I ran into one of my best friends from childhood, Jill. She invited me over to her house to meet a couple of guy friends; she was quick to warn me that Dennis was hers. As I mentioned previously, I was praying for a Christian husband to complete my life, so I happily accepted her invitation to check out the possibilities. It was there that I met a young man named Roger Vann.

Roger was tall, thin, and had a crop of thick strawberry-blonde hair. He subsequently asked me out on a date and we began learning about each other and just having fun. It definitely wasn't love at first sight, but we enjoyed one another's company and, eventually, he won my heart. His love for the things of God attracted me to him more than his looks or demeanor.

3

Roger's Story

ROGER WAS RAISED IN A FUNDAMENTAL Christian home. His parents were poor, but churchgoers—good Christian people. He was a very likeable kid and loved to go to church. He memorized Bible verses and was a quiet, nice little boy. His parents farmed in Wisconsin for a time and then decided to look for a better life by entering into the job force. His father held a series of jobs that resulted in moving the family often.

At first, Roger enjoyed school; that would change. In first grade, he showed a spark of promise when he reached the top of the class in spelling and reading, but just as he was beginning to get his legs under him, he had to move again before the end of the year. This constant disruption in his life proved to be very detrimental and added to his always feeling unsettled and disconnected.

By the time he was in the third grade, he had attended seven elementary schools as his father continued uprooting the family to look for work. Roger was feeling more and more insecure and was often times ostracized by the other kids. They cruelly teased him because he wasn't able to dress as well as they did, or take family vacations to far away destinations. As soon as they found out he was poor, nobody wanted to be his friend. Although he was a bright student and liked to talk, he resisted being told what to do. In kindergarten, he was often punished for talking when he wasn't supposed to, and the teacher took excessive measures such as locking him in the dark coatroom. The crime didn't fit the punishment, but back then the kindergartner had no one to advocate for him. His frustration grew.

One day, his family went to hear Billy Graham preach at the Minnesota State Fairgrounds. Even at the tender age of five, Roger was very excited because he had heard him preach before and Graham was somewhat of a celebrity. When the altar call was given, he popped up out of his seat and began to run down to the platform below. "If you want Jesus Christ as your personal Savior, come forward now," Graham encouraged the people. His father rushed after him, "Wait a minute, Roger, where do you think you're going?" "I'm going to give my heart to Jesus!" he told him. "You come back to your seat. You don't have to go down there." "Yes, I do; I want to be saved!" Roger's father forced him back into his seat quenching the pull of the Holy Spirit in his little boy. Roger was greatly disappointed, but he repeated the sinner's prayer anyway and, at that moment, determined he would be God's little man and would someday be a preacher.

On Sunday afternoons, he would go into his back yard with his Bible, gather the neighborhood children, and, even though he couldn't read, told them, "If you want to go to heaven then you have to accept Jesus." Most of his little congregation didn't know what heaven was and, truth be told, he probably didn't either. But that didn't matter to him; he just wanted to preach to anyone who would listen!

At twelve, after years of being excluded, he began to dread going to school because he never felt like he fit in. His mannerisms were often times misunderstood as he struggled to be accepted in school and at home. Instead of compassion and understanding, his father disciplined him vigorously thinking he was just being rebellious. He failed to recognize the pain that was deep within him. In his heart of hearts, Roger desperately wanted to be good and feel the acceptance of his father; however; he often found that good was never good enough where he was concerned. To add insult to injury, most everyone he knew, inside and outside of church, was upper and middle-class. They never missed an opportunity to remind him that he was poor and therefore must be of less value. He always felt segregated from his peers. Deep disappointment and anger began to take root inside.

One time, he attended a youth social put on by the church. Everyone was asked to bring something to share, so he brought a bag of potato chips: the most economical kind. The other kids brought attractive trays of food—sandwiches, cookies, and name-brand snacks. At the end of the evening, the food was eaten to the final crumb, but his cheap potato chips remained untouched in the bag. He was emotionally devastated and embarrassed by the knowledge of his poverty and the feeling that, again, he wasn't good enough.

Roger continued to try to seek for solace and acceptance within the Christian community, but time and time again what he got was rejection and unkind remarks making him feel like he didn't belong; he was beneath them and unworthy of their friendship. It's sad that church people didn't understand that the Jesus they supposedly served came for the poor and broken, and He harshly criticized those who exalted themselves above others. The kids from the upper-class homes always sat together on the church bus while Roger would find a seat by himself and stare out the window. One day something snapped; he had had enough and decided that he didn't want to fit in anymore. All Christians were phonies and hypocrites. At that moment, he felt a burning deep inside him that was to follow him for many years thereafter, and set him on a path of self-destruction.

Roger's father, as previously mentioned, was gone so much that he never bonded with his son and viewed him as a rebellious teen-ager in need of the hand of correction. His method of discipline was to use a strap on him, deprive him of privileges, and restrict his ac-tivities. Roger's deep-seated unhappiness was always interpreted as disobedience. Their relationship was fractured beyond repair.

Longing to be accepted and miserably unhappy, he searched for acceptance outside his family and church and discovered that al-though the kids at church rejected him, the kids on the street did not. This is where he found full acceptance; whether he was poor or not, the playing field was evened out. Sooner or later, rejection sends people on a quest to find the place where they will fit in, good or bad!

Just then, the family moved to a duplex on the east side of St. Paul owned by a family from the local church. They lived downstairs and the Vanns upstairs. Roger made friends right away with their son Dennis, who was his same age. Both sets of parents were Christians, so they became fast friends. The relationship between Roger and his father continued to deteriorate day by day. He could never live up to the expectations his father placed on him and finally Roger gave up trying. He succumbed to the inevitable. His frustration and disap-pointment escalated when his dad said words that never left him,

"You just want to goof around, Roger," he accused, "You want to be a bum, that's all." These words would play many times like a broken record throughout his future, and the enemy of his soul planted more negative seeds into his psyche. The garden of his heart was being planted with seeds of pain, rejection, and worthlessness. What once was fertile, innocent ground was now growing out of control with destructive weeds choking out God's beautiful plan for his life.

Satan was busy forming his own plan of destruction as Roger's anger grew. The downward spiral took him to places he never dreamed he would go. He began hanging around pool halls, perfecting his game and receiving his worldly education. It was there that he was introduced to alcohol and the seedy side of society. His temper grew from anger into uncontrollable rage to the point that any little thing would set him off: a word, a look, anything. He picked fights and beat people to within inches their life if they crossed him. His nickname became, "Crazy Reggie," Finally, he was accepted… for being bad!

His bitterness and fury continued to deepen, not because of the poverty anymore, because he could always steal whatever he needed, but because he still experienced the thing he hated most—not fitting in. Whether it was perceived or real, he couldn't shake the gnawing idea that he wasn't as worthwhile as other people. His temper became uncontrollable and was a hair trigger. He once put a man in the hospital because he interrupted his pool game. The guy stood near him and heckled him about paying him the ten dollars Roger owed him. Roger ignored him until he had enough and annoyance turned into rage. He leapt over the pool table and began punching him, all the while yelling, "I'm going to kill you, I'm going to kill you!" His buddies pulled him off the man to keep him from going past the point of no return. They didn't want him to be arrested for murder. Later, Roger found out that "Tweetie," never fully recovered and ended up with brain damage. The worst tragedy of all is that he didn't care. Rage grew stronger.

Unbeknown to Roger and Dennis, two mothers were praying for their sons who had both strayed from under the protection of their loving God. Roger was drinking heavily by this time and his only source of income was generated by successfully playing pool and winning every time! He was considered the young version of "Minnesota Fats." He not only became well known in St. Paul for his pool playing expertise, but also for his temper. He was subsequently thrown out of almost every bar, club, and pool hall around. Soon, no one would play him for money because of his "pool shark" and "Crazy Reggie" reputation.

He never seemed to be able to hold down a normal job, so playing pool was his only source of income. He lived in a $45-a-month, furnished apartment going nowhere in life. He spent every penny he made on his addictions. One day, as Roger was complaining that his head hurt, a guy he was acquainted with from the pool hall invited him out for a drink and introduced him to some pills that would "cure the headache." He slammed them down by the fistful, which sent him reeling. He now was officially part of the drug culture and his best friends became drunks, druggies, and killers with prison records.

One day, Roger's barber suggested he should join the Air Force where he could make lots of money playing in tournaments. Roger was secretly starting to look at maybe changing his life for the better, as he began feeling he was headed down a path of total destruction, but the possibility of hustling "ignorant men," who were unaware of his pool-playing prowess and reputation, was appealing. He enlisted and was accepted into the Air Force. At first it became quite easy to relieve guys of their paychecks. Unfortunately, it didn't take long for them to figure out how good he was. Soon, no one on base would play him, so he decided to find greener pastures and sneak into town to find more unsuspecting prospects.

He began getting into a lot of trouble as his old habits of fighting, drugging, and carousing began to surface. He was so exhausted that while he was on duty as a military policeman, he was caught sleeping on his watch. This happened more than once, and Roger was ultimately stripped of his rank and threatened with a dishonorable discharge if his behavior didn't stop. He didn't care. He decided he would have to become more discreet and continued his drug usage, biding his time until he was released from the service. A chilling thought crossed his mind that he had not been sober for a single twenty-four hour period in the three-and-a-half years he had been on duty in London. He ended up with an honorable discharge, but only by the skin of his teeth.

Back in the States, Roger was walking down the street and, quite by chance, ran into Dennis coming out of a bar. They had a brief conversation about where the years had taken them. They parted ways and didn't see one another until quite some time later. Roger made a mental note of the fact that Dennis, too, was deep into alcoholism.

Post service, Roger severed his relationship with his father and continued his "job" selling drugs to young kids and hippies. He spiraled even deeper into his private hell of drugs and poisonous behavior: all of which took a huge toll on his mind and body. He was starving and couldn't sleep. One day, he looked into the mirror, and staring back at him was the hideous face of Satan. Fear gripped his heart, and he immediately became paranoid and began hearing voices. One by one, his druggie friends were committing suicide, dying of overdoses, or ending up in jail. He didn't want to end up like that but couldn't stop. He was so burned out and felt he was nearing the end of his rope. He had an ominous sense that he was close to death himself, and began to remembering how much he had once loved and wanted to serve God as a child.

Just then, he recalled a recent conversation he had with his mother. She said, "Dennis is a Christian now, Roger."

Frantically, he reached for the phone to call his friend. Dennis picked up the phone. "Thank God," Roger thought.

"Why don't you meet me at my mom's at four o'clock tomorrow; she is having a Bible study there," Dennis said.

Roger was disappointed because he desperately wanted to meet Dennis immediately, thinking he might not make it to the next day, but he finally agreed to his friend's suggestion.

Roger's parents no longer shared the duplex and had moved a couple blocks away from Dennis' mom's house. He had some trepidation as he sheepishly approached the front door. He wondered what she would think, what she would say. Would she put him on the spot? She came to the door and invited him in. For the first time in a long time he felt the warmth of God's love as he was offered a cup of coffee and a great meal: something he hadn't had in a long time. It was only four o'clock and the meeting didn't start until seven o'clock. He became Pearl's captive audience. She lovingly told him he needed to give his life back to the Lord. That night, during the Bible study, testimonies were given and scripture was read. The words he heard were like old forgotten friends. Dennis looked happy and healthy, unlike when they had bumped into each other many months ago, when Dennis had staggered out of a bar and onto the street. This spoke volumes to Roger.

After the meeting, Dennis dropped him off at his cockroach-infested apartment with blood-spattered walls and drunks in the hallway. He fell to his knees by his bed. "O Lord Jesus, take me back," he whispered. "Please give me another chance. I really know living for you is the right way. I really see it this time. Honest I do."

He started to cry, thinking of all he had lost, of the pain and anguish he had caused so many, of how he had destroyed himself. "O God, forgive me. Please forgive me. I want to live for you from now on! I really do!" He fell into bed with a sense of relief, and for the first time in a long time, sleep came easily. When he awoke the next morning, he knew something wonderful had happened to him.

Dennis became his emissary. He called Roger right away and insisted on picking him up for church. A little of the old Roger tried to make an excuse as to why he couldn't go, but Dennis wouldn't hear of it and insisted that he get ready because he was on his way to get him. Roger always wore long-sleeved shirts to hide the track marks on his arms and worried that he wouldn't be accepted by the church people just like when he was a kid.

That Sunday, Roger made a public confession of his faith in Christ as people prayed over him in a powerful way. He felt as though he had been on a long journey and now he had come home! The residuals of his drug usage however, were still evident as he had a hard time conversing normally: his speech hesitant and labored, his thoughts scattered. One weekend, he and Dennis attended a retreat. The speaker, sensing Roger had been a drug user, asked if he could pray over him that God would heal and restore his mind so that he could be the preacher He had called him to be. "Father, Satan has affected Roger's mind, but now I pray in the name of your Son Jesus, that Roger's mind be healed," he said.

Suddenly his voice became like charges of electricity flying all around him. There was an explosion within him, and his ears popped as though they had been filled with water. He gasped as he felt the warmth of Jesus' hands on his head. He knew that God was touching him and that something sinister and awful was leaving him. He suddenly felt cleansed, as though he had been in a long hot shower and the heavy weight had been lifted from his shoulders. He felt free!

At that time, Dennis was sharing a one-bedroom basement apartment with a guy from his work. "Move in with us," he offered, knowing Roger would never make it unless he was in a decent place surrounded by others who loved and served God. Dennis's roommate had agreed, but now they had to meet all the objectives Roger had when he mildly protested that it might be too crowded with three of them in such a tiny space. They finally convinced him that it would be the best thing for him. Secretly, he was grateful and their couch became his bed.

The three began having Bible studies and invited all their friends and neighbors. Roger was so excited about his new life that he called all his old friends and told them what had happened to him. They were skeptical but slowly, one-by-one began to come to Jesus. Just like Roger, it became imperative that they needed to move out of the hell holes they were living in and away from people who would tempt them to go back to the old life. Three became four when a new convert named Dave moved in. It became so crowded they decided it was time to look for a larger place. They saw an ad in the paper for a house that was up for rent, and although they didn't have any money, they prayed in faith and approached the owner, sharing their vision with him. God moved upon the heart of that man and he agreed to let them rent it.

The home was spacious and located on Portland Avenue just outside downtown Minneapolis; thus, it became known as the "Portland House." The guys gladly slept on the floor and began praying every day for the household things they needed. They prayed for furniture, dishes, bedding, and, marvelously, all of the items came in free of charge. People would call them up on the telephone, "Hello, Roger? Listen, we have this old refrigerator in our basement..." Or, "Do you need any curtains or dishes?" God used His people to answer their prayers. Tuesday night Bible studies began in the living room where they fellowshipped, prayed, and studied the Word of God.

Roger began receiving invitations to give his testimony at some of the local churches. He would talk about his deliverance and freedom from drugs. As a result of the Holy Spirit moving on hearts, many people gave their hearts and lives to the Lord. "If God can set me free, He can set you free, too," he told them.

They continued to invite outsiders to the Tuesday night Bible studies. To their surprise, the kids from the streets streamed like melting snow into the house each week, giving their hearts and lives over to the Lord! At the end of each Bible study, those who had accepted Jesus went downstairs to the prayer room and received special prayer and counseling.

The little band of God's warriors, armed with their life-changing message, went to parks and other places where people congregated, played their guitars, and witnessed about the love of Jesus to anyone who would listen. People did listen and began to flock to their meetings. The Bible studies grew until they had almost ninety kids packed into the house every week. God's spirit moved mightily!

Revival was sweeping across America at that time and was referred to as the "Jesus People" movement. The hippie culture was finding Jesus as never before and these two young men from Soul's Harbor felt the calling of God upon their lives to reach that unchurched segment of society. They wanted the culture they had managed to survive, to find redemption, peace, and healing of both mind and body just as they had. Roger and Dennis decided to make an appointment to meet with their pastor, Reverend Peterson, to explain how they felt God calling them into a ministry for this purpose and these people. "Rev," as everyone affectionately called him, gave them his blessing and encouraged them to follow the Lord into whatever it was He had for them.

Roger and Dennis began to pray and contemplate God's plan and next step for their future ministry. They were aware of many who criticized them and questioned their ability and qualifications to pastor their little rag-tagged band of brothers and sisters, but they kept their eyes on the One who called them and continued to pray for His direction. "If God be for us, who can be against us" was the scripture they were inspired with.

4

Two Become One

ROGER HAD A JOB AT A VENDING COMPANY, which took much of his time away from the home, the young people, and the ministry. He began to fast and pray, asking the Lord to direct him as to whether or not he should leave his job and pursue full time ministry. The answer was "yes." We were dating then and my parents weren't happy about the prospect of their daughter marrying someone with no job.

When he finally worked up the courage to ask me to marry him, he said to me, "I want to be a preacher, Jackie, I want to evangelize the world and win souls for Christ. I believe that's what God has called me to do in this life."

"I believe that too," I said, "and I'd like very much to be the wife of a preacher."

On April 18, 1970, we were married. We said, "'til death do us part." For the next sixteen years, those vows were intact. I believed with all my heart that our marriage would grow stronger with each anniversary year and that we would grow old together. One never knows exactly how things will turn out because, as we all know, life sometimes throws us a curve. I anticipated great success because I viewed Roger and me as a team! I thought that no matter what we were faced with, we would be able to present a formidable barrier against any adversity as long as God was at the center of our lives.

We both loved God and wanted to serve Him, embracing everything His plan entailed for us no matter where that took us in life. We fully trusted that God could and would provide for our every need. I supported Roger's calling and together our faith grew day-by-day as we experienced our Lord's provision. We felt His presence as we fellowshipped with Him during those fledgling years. I remember how little money we had to live on, but our love for each other, and God's miraculous ways of meeting our needs (supernaturally sometimes), sustained us. Our faith soared many times; when we were down to the last morsel of food and money, we would get on our knees and pray that God would supply. Guess what? He always did, right on time.

I had confidence in God and my husband. I respected Roger as a man of God: dedicated and consecrated to His calling. He was humble and always so grateful for being set free from his drug addiction and his troubled past that he was convinced others like him could have that same freedom. He was passionate about God and sensed He had something special for him to do. He spent hours on his knees, in the presence of the Lord, waiting for His direction regarding the ministry.

The day he gave his life to Jesus, he bankrupted himself and gave God everything he had. That's one of the things I loved most about him. I was committed to being the woman supporting my husband, and doing my part to further his vision. I was willing to experience the blessings and the hardships, whatever came with it. I was happy and proud to be me, and to serve the Lord alongside of him.

My parents, however, were somewhat dismayed that we lived on so little and couldn't wrap their minds around Roger's belief that God would supply "all" our needs. My father once said, "Roger is so heavenly minded, he's no earthly good." No one knew what was ahead for us, but God did!

Dennis married Jill and they became house parents to the new converts at the "Portland House." Each week, Roger and Dennis continued taking turns giving their testimonies and preaching whatever they felt the Holy Spirit impressing them to talk about. It was always heartfelt and anointed. God's love flowed. They didn't believe in a holier-than-thou type of preaching but felt that in sharing their own personal struggles, problems, and victories, people could better identify with their own issues.

The Kingdom of God was growing daily with young people abandoning their destructive lifestyles and embracing the powerful message of John 3:16. The kingdom of Satan, on the other hand, suffered lethal blows time after time. I picture him rallying his troops with great flurry to try and stop the hemorrhaging and launch an assault. It would serve us well to remember that it may not be today, tomorrow, next month, or next year, but Satan is always on the prowl waiting for a weak moment to take advantage of us. He is very patient.

Because of the explosion of new converts, Dennis and Roger felt they should expand the ministry to provide a house for girls. Prayers went up and God miraculously provided the finances. It soon became reality. So, after we got married, Roger and I decided to move into the third floor of the attic of the "Park House." This space obviously was intended for storage, but we decided we would do what we needed to do to make it our little home. Our double bed and small dresser was all we could fit into the tiny bedroom. It was so cramped I found it easier to get dressed in the bathroom or kitchenette that was up there.

It was unspeakably hot in the summer. Roger got a window air-conditioner and installed it in our bedroom window. What a relief. We thought, *This is opulence at its best!* We were so grateful and thankful for everything and anything. The kitchen had a linoleum floor, a single corner sink, and at the opposite end, an apartment-type gas stove. We were thrilled that we had an old, working refrigerator. There were three small windows, about a foot off the floor, which overlooked Park Avenue. The bathroom had a bathtub, sink with a mirror, and a toilet. We were blessed that we didn't have to share the bathroom on the second floor with the thirteen girls that lived below us.

Most of the time, we ate upstairs in our apartment and had quiet conversation about the day's happenings. This little corner of the world was also where Roger would take the first hour of his day to get on his knees and pray. He wanted to grow his relationship with God and be filled with His power. The only thing he wanted to do was to preach God's Word and see people's lives changed by it. He talked many times about the fact that he vividly remembered how he had felt having been given a new chance at life. He said it was an indescribable feeling and again wanted that for others.

There were times we gathered together downstairs in the main dining room with the girls (and guys) to celebrate a birthday or reconnect over a meal. It was rewarding to share food and conversation as we enjoyed good fellowship, even if sometimes it was mixed with drama, which it usually was. It always took time for a new person moving in to adjust to the routine and personalities of those who were already there, but eventually they learned to work things out and became a family. Deep down, they were good kids who needed love, direction, and a large encounter with God. It was exhilarating to see the transformation in their lives.

In the late 60s, meetings were held one night a week at the girls' house on Park Avenue. The gatherings grew from 15, to 20, to 35, then one day to 75, 80, and then 100. It showed no signs of stopping. People from all over the Twin Cities attended the weekly meeting. The living room filled up first. We moved the large dining room table off to one side to give us more space to set folding chairs. The extra wide staircase going up to second floor was filled with people sitting shoulder to shoulder on each step, trying to fit their feet between the arms of those sitting in front of them. They spilled out of the house, onto the porch, out on the front steps, and then to the front lawn. If you didn't get there early, you didn't get in. It filled up very quickly.

Low and behold, while we were living in these cramped quarters, we found out our first child was on the way. Darcy Faye entered our lives and our limited space on October 21, 1971. We were at a quandary as to where to put her. Behind the bathroom was a small room just large enough for her crib. It also had a tiny closet for her clothes. In spite of the lack of space, it was a refuge for our family. We were so happy to have our beautiful little baby girl, even though she cried incessantly for eight months, which took its toll on our nervous systems. In order for her to stop bellowing, I had to rip a sheet into strips and tie her to me so I that I could do my housework, cook, and go about the daily chores.

Before we were married, Roger had mentioned to me that he really wasn't interested in having children. I promptly told him, in no uncertain terms, that I wouldn't marry him then because I loved and wanted kids. As soon as Darcy was born, he changed his mind and was happy and proud of his precious gift from God. Right then and there, I was determined to be the best mother I could to Darcy and any other children that might be in our future. I immersed myself in motherhood. I knew being the wife of a pastor was important, but now my daughter took priority over everything else. My philosophy was God first, family second, and ministry third. Roger however, had his priorities in a different order, as we would find out in the days to come.

The living room prayer meetings continued for five years and as the word spread, the crowds grew even bigger as God moved in the hearts and lives of the people. One night, the City of Minneapolis sent the fire marshal to one of our meetings and he proceeded to threaten to shut us down because we were breaking the fire code with the number of people we had crammed in the house. It became evident to us that God was moving us on. We needed to trust Him to provide us with a larger facility. We began praying, and by faith collected contributions from our financially poor little congregation of misfits (according to society) to purchase a church building. We were led to a former Christian Science Church on 15th Avenue South in Minneapolis, and scraped enough together to give them a down payment.

On February 9, 1972, Roger and Dennis put together a list of charter members (required by the state) and founded Jesus People Church. What we didn't know then was that in a few short years the name "Jesus People Church" would become known nationwide, and that we would be one of the largest churches in the five-state area. Ronald, Mark, James, and Michael were selected to be the first elders for our church. Even though they weren't too elderly, and were more hippy-style wise than most people expect elders to be today, they loved God with all their hearts and wanted to serve Him in any way they could. People continued to come in droves.

A couple years later, we were again faced with the same problem; we were bursting at the seams. Roger and Dennis did everything they could do to try and make room for people. They utilized all the rooms in the building and squeezed more pews up in the balcony to accommodate the hungry crowd. People were lining up into the parking lot trying to get inside. Again, the fire department showed up and said we needed to downsize the amount of people or they would close us down. In our minds, turning people away that were coming to see Jesus move and giving their lives over to Him was not an option! Revival was alive and healthy. Every service was packed with excited people who anticipated a mighty move of God within themselves and others.

Once again, in 1974, God prompted Roger and Dennis to look for an even larger facility. They sought the Lord and were led to the First Church of Christ Scientist on 24th and Nicollet Avenue. God continued to move in miraculous ways, and the crowds kept growing. Now we had evolved into a congregation that consisted of professional businessmen, young and old, long-haired hippies, children, and people from all walks of life. God's spirit was felt by everyone and it was as if they couldn't get enough. Money was not an issue.

5

A Place of Our Own

AFTER TWO YEARS OF LIVING IN THE ATTIC at the Park House, it was time to think about purchasing a home for our family. The air conditioner couldn't keep up with the sweltering heat during those extremely hot summer nights, and we grew tired of hauling our mattress downstairs in order to sleep on the living room floor with people coming and going through the front door.

A Christian businessman from our church decided to help us obtain a government-guaranteed, low-income loan. He even gave us the down payment for a little two-bedroom bungalow near Minnehaha Park in South Minneapolis. It was small and had no garage, but to us it was a mansion. We couldn't believe it was ours. It had a fenced in, well-manicured backyard where Darcy loved to go and play. There was a small garden and sandbox off to the side of the property. I loved to garden while Darcy entertained herself digging in the sand. We were so grateful to have our "us only" house with normal-sized rooms and a real kitchen with a full sized range. I relished it even though it was only nine hundred square feet.

It was such a luxury to be able to put Darcy in her own little room for the night. It was then that Roger and I would talk about our plans, dreams, and expectations without disturbing our sleeping daughter. I looked forward to those evenings when Roger would come home and we could be together after his busy day of helping others. Often, work took precedence over our family time. Even so, I was content to mother Darcy, keep a tidy house, garden, and cook.

We loved our first home and made many wonderful memories while there. It was so peaceful. We were living life, enjoying total contentment, when out of nowhere, we were dealt a potentially fatal blow. On December 10, 1972, a few months after we moved in, Roger was diagnosed with testicular cancer. When the doctor walked into the room with the results of his tests, he told him, in no uncertain terms, to go home and get his affairs in order because he had only six months to two years at best to live. I wasn't there when he got the news, but I sensed the fear and anxiety in his words as he sat me down to tell me. It was so surreal listening to the words and trying to process what I heard. Every emotion in me was on high alert. It was bizarre. For a few moments as I sat stunned, I felt myself going into denial and subconsciously rejecting the message. At first, I thought it was a hideous joke. Then he told me his surgery was scheduled for Monday.

Roger was only twenty-seven, and I couldn't conceive of the idea that God would allow him to be taken away from me, Darcy, and the church ministry prematurely. For what reason? It was not possible; I would not, I could not believe it. I reasoned: God would not have called us to minister, to experience the powerful Holy Spirit-inspired movement we'd been involved in, and then take Roger. Where was the victory in that? Besides, he wouldn't tear our lives apart like that. This didn't line up with God's Word and this was not His plan for us, I determined. He called us to preach His Word, He provided for all our needs, and we were seeing new converts totally changed and serving God.

Our faith was being tested to a degree we hadn't experienced before. One thing was for sure and obvious to us; Satan had leveled his attack and the fight was on. He thought he had hit the bull's-eye with this one, and I knew at that moment we needed to put on the armor of God and fight against the evil enemy who was out to steal, kill, and destroy us and God's vibrant work. His strategy was to attack our thoughts, our bodies, and our spirit to try and weaken our resolve to serve the Lord and thwart the ministry.

The following Sunday morning, Roger announced to the congregation that he had been diagnosed with cancer and was going in for surgery the next day. He humbly asked for their prayers. Everyone gathered around him, as if positioning soldiers for a battle, and cried out to God, lifting their pastor to Him and asking for the healing of his body. Their faith soared as they believed for this miracle.

Not only was Roger's life at stake, but we were without health insurance with which to cover medical bills, and our bank account was dragging the bottom of the barrel: another thing to trust God for. We drew from the past and remembered all the times He provided for our every need when we had nothing. He had always been and always would be our El Shaddai—God our provider! The congregants decided to take up a free will offering for us and we stood there stunned at the love, compassion, and generosity of people as they gave all they could. We marched forward, trying to believe without doubt or wavering that He held us securely in His capable hands.

This is never easy, but clinging to scriptures pertaining to healing and the attributes of God, we launched out into the unknown.

As I walked alongside the hospital cart, I kept reassuring my husband that he was going to be OK, that God was with him, watching over him, and guiding the surgeon's hands. We hoped that the report would good, but after the operation, we were told that the type and aggressiveness of the cancer was the worst possible kind. Because of this, the doctors pressured Roger to let them perform lymph node biopsies to see if it had metastasized. I imagined Satan wringing his hands in sheer joy, thinking he was going to take Roger out and end his vision to honor God and work as hard as he could to bring everyone within the reach of his voice to the foot of the cross.

Roger made his decision and, much to the doctors' dismay and council against not doing it, decided to stand on his faith. This was where the Red Sea would either be parted or it wouldn't, and it was time to exercise his faith in the One he preached about, studied, depended upon, and believed in to confirm his calling. He was going to completely put his trust and life in the Master's hands and say "Thy will be done." He declined the biopsy tests. There are so many crossroads in life that beg us to make a decision based on what we believe and who we believe in. Because we can't see the future, we have to rely on God's Word and His directive.

After his proclamation, I began to speak words of faith into Roger. "We don't have to buy time from the doctors, we'll trust God. Roger, I believe He will heal you. I just believe it. I know you're going to be OK," I proclaimed. Thinking back on that now, I can honestly say I never once feared for our future or that God wouldn't heal him.

We held each other's hands and prayed together, and at that moment I knew that I knew that he was healed and would be alive for years to come. The enemy began relentlessly attacking Roger's mind not only through his own thoughts but the fearful words spoken to him by other people. Doubt began to rear its ugly head as his thoughts turned to, maybe, just maybe he wouldn't be healed. We knew Satan wasn't planning on giving up easily. As Roger battled through negative thoughts that would be coming faster than they would be deflected, he would confess his faith in God and believe His word. Occasionally, he would verbalize a doubt and as soon as it came out of his mouth, I replied, "You are healed! You are going to continue to minister. We will go on together. Great things are ahead for us!"

We would stand together, hand in hand, trusting and speaking out loud the scripture that Jesus spoke; "By my stripes, you are healed." Oh, there were plenty of naysayers and accusers who tried to tell us that because we had started a renegade church for hippies and rebels from the streets that God was punishing us. That just made us fight that much harder as we looked up every scripture pertaining to healing and painstakingly focused on what God said and not what others had dumped on us. I continually told Roger, "Don't give up; I won't ever give up on you. Neither will Jesus."

A few short weeks after Roger's surgery, God began to put it in my heart that we should have another child. We had a discussion with the cancer specialists about the possibility of our being able to have more children and they were quite sure that the possibility was "slim to none." I put my inclinations on the shelf. About six months later, something within me again began to suggest we should attempt to have another baby. It wasn't something I had planned but there was such an urgency deep within my spirit I knew it had to do with what we were going through. It would be confirmation that Roger was healed. "Roger, I think we need another baby," I said boldly.

"Are you kidding me? Are you sure this would be the right thing to do? What if…." He kept going on and on.

I replied emphatically, "You are healed! We need another baby to complete our family," I announced with assurance and confidence. I was determined and I now knew God was not going to take him home. We would continue to go forward under the umbrella and blessings of our God.

Our beautiful baby boy, Jeremiah Earl Vann, was born December 2, 1973. He was our sign that God was with us! Roger was then about fifteen months out from his surgery and as far as we were concerned, God performed the miracle we and our church family had prayed for. Following his birth, we did make the decision to have my tubes tied because we felt we had our perfect little family.

We were now beginning to feel rather cramped in our little house. Darcy was four and Jeremiah two when the bedroom they shared began to close in on them. We decided it was time to move into a larger home that would give us more space and growing room. We began to pray and make some plans. We looked for a lot in different parts of the suburbs and finally decided that Plymouth was a perfect community. Finances were much better now, and Roger and I were grateful to the Lord for His provision making it possible for us to begin building our beautiful tri-level home. The builders we selected were contractors who attended our church and we trusted them to be good stewards of our money. They worked hard to get us the best prices on materials such as flooring products, hardware, carpeting, etc. It took quite a few months to complete and was finally finished in January of 1976.

We each had our wish lists. In the large family room, Roger wanted oak tongue-and-groove paneling with a massive brick fireplace, which held a huge rough-sawn wood mantle above, and it turned out just as he had hoped. The family room then extended through toward the back of the house to a 16 x 16 foot porch or sitting room. It had lovely big windows on three sides, with a huge picture window in the middle. Roger claimed this as "his" space early on.

Up the stairs a half level was the kitchen that led into the formal dining room, and adjacent to that was the living room. The front windows overlooked a beautiful, treed yard that gave much needed shade during the hot summer months. Darcy and Jeremiah weren't allowed in the living room as that was the "peanut butter and jelly free" zone. There were plenty of other places for them to scatter toys and be normal kids.

Up another half level, were the bedrooms and bathrooms. Darcy and Jeremiah's rooms had a bathroom between them that was accessible by both. Our master bedroom suite was across the hall. It was huge, and had French doors that opened up into a large office where Roger could study and prepare his sermons without being disturbed. North and west windows overlooked the backyard, making it restful and secluded. The closet space was especially enjoyable to me after having had very little in the Park House and our first home. I was ecstatic that our new bedroom had one whole wall of double closets, albeit Roger's suits took up most of it. We also had a ceramic-tiled full bathroom. We almost didn't know how to react to such luxury.

My wish list had to do with one of the most important rooms of the house—the kitchen. The kitchen was bi-level; the upper level was the prep and cooking area and the lower was an informal eating area where we enjoyed most of our meals. Out of our kitchen wafted wonderful smells and foods that speak love from a wife and mother to her family. My kitchen had state-of-the-art appliances that made me feel that I could feed five thousand if necessary. This was where I worked my culinary magic to my heart's content. I was really into cooking healthy foods for my family, and the kitchen was fully equipped to encourage me to be able to do that. Looking out of the sliding glass doors from the lower level eating area, was a beautiful patio with a gas grill. We really enjoyed picnicking outside on the patio when the weather was nice.

As I mentioned before, I preferred to serve my family healthy foods, but Roger wasn't much into sprouts, homemade pumpkin pies, and bread made from unbleached flour. His menu of choice was meat, potatoes, and fast foods, but I thought maybe I could change his mind over time. I continued to cook lots of fresh vegetables and new healthy recipes to try them out on him and the kids. He protested vehemently, asking for "normal" food and resisted my attempt to raise the standard.

The backyard was perfect for the kids and our dog Suelee to play in. Suelee was an adorable little mutt. We called her our Heinz 57 because we weren't sure just what mix she was. She had large brown eyes, medium-long hair, and a lower jaw overbite. Her tail was long and the hair on it fell down like pineapple leaves. The family would say she was so ugly she was cute. She had a wonderful low-key personality and was excellent with the kids. She had one bad habit however. One time, I had grilled a beautiful steak to perfection. I called Roger to come down for dinner and set the plate on the table. I then went back to the kitchen to bring out the rest of the dinner. Before Roger made it downstairs, Suelee grabbed and totally consumed his steak in seconds flat, and licked the plate clean. That plate left no sign that there had been even a morsel of food on it! Needless to say, she wasn't very cute at that particular moment, and Roger made his disgust known in no uncertain terms. It wasn't funny then, but every time I think about it now, I have to chuckle. She was like a bolt of lightning that hit and ran. From then on, I had to watch her like a hawk any time food was within her reach.

A few years later, we added another member to our family: Kizzy, a beautiful Doberman pinscher. We had a doctor living next door who was less than enthusiastic about the idea of a Doberman living next to his family. In order to not alienate them, we decided to fence our backyard to keep peace. They always remained cordial, and stayed a respectable distance away from us even though I tried to assure them Kizzy was harmless.

Kizzy was thoroughly obedience-trained and I enjoyed showing off her skills at dog shows throughout the Twin Cities. Sometimes she would win a blue, red, or yellow ribbon but, truthfully, I didn't care if she won anything. If we did happened to win a ribbon, it was just frosting on the cake. The main reason we competed was so that I could spend some special time with her. We both enjoyed and had fun doing it.

I was a runner and Kizzy became my jogging buddy for ten years. She knew the routes as well as I did. Even to this day, I vividly remember our early morning jogs being filled with the fresh, damp smells of the season, hearing the birds singing, and the muffled sound of my feet hitting the ground. When I would let her off her leash, she bounded into the fields, jumping through tall weeds and grass like a deer. Then, when she was ready, she would make her way back to my side. I derived a great sense of well-being and serenity during those runs as it became my time to spend alone with God, surrounding myself in His creation without any interruption. I relished and cherished every moment. My life, I reflect, was filled with trying to be the best wife I could, the best mom I could, and the best homemaker I could. I cooked, cleaned, and looked after my little family with great passion and was perfectly content to do so.

Our son Jeremiah was a brilliant little boy that was in need of two full time parents! He was very active. He got into everything and, on a daily basis, challenged my ability to keep track of what he was up to. As Roger and I were in the process of unpacking at the new house, my goal was to get anything that was dangerous up and out of the way of the kids. We were there only a matter of hours when we discovered that Jeremiah had completely dismantled the entire fireplace—frame, doors, and insides—within minutes while our backs were turned. To this day, I can't figure out how a two-year old could accomplish that task. As adults, we had a difficult time trying to reassemble it. Shortly after that fiasco, Jeremiah appeared to be focused on playing with his toys in the family room, so I busied myself unpacking the kitchen things.

I didn't realize he had quietly slipped away and had gone down into the basement. All of a sudden, he appeared next to me and caught my attention when I heard him crunching on something. "Let me see…open your mouth." I was horrified to discover he had gotten into a box of light bulbs that were packed away in one of the moving boxes, and evidently while playing with them, broke one. He decided to put a piece in his mouth and was chewing on it when he returned to me. I quickly looked inside his mouth to check for bleeding and, thank God, didn't see anything. My relief turned into panic; did he swallow any glass shards? I immediately called the doctor and asked him what to do. He told me to give him plenty of bread to eat and check all his bowel movements for evidence. For the next three days, I picked through his diapers and pulled out some unbelievable pieces that he had ingested, but, miraculously, with no ill effects that we could see.

I carefully washed off each piece and taped them into his baby book, so I would have proof of the protection God afforded my son.

To this day, it gives me shivers when I think of what could have happened. When I took him in for a checkup and the doctor saw the sizes of the pieces and how jagged the pieces were, he couldn't believe that his mouth and gums weren't cut and that his esophagus and bowel hadn't suffered any permanent damage. I continued to watch him closely for any pain or bleeding, but nothing presented itself. Truly it was a miracle!

The antics continued. When he was about three-and-a-half, I went to open the basement door and it almost fell on me. Jeremiah had removed the two lower pins: the ones he could reach. Even though Jeremiah had an endearing personality, and an innocent look about him, it seemed he was always in places he wasn't supposed to be and doing things he wasn't supposed to be doing. The older he got, the more trouble he got into both at home and at the church. He was the pastor's son, yet I was the one, not Roger, who was the recipient of the backlash from the church people and our neighbors regarding his out-of-control behavior. He kept me in a virtual whirl-wind. He required so much of my attention that his sister, Darcy, was left in the dust.

The older he got, the bigger the offenses became. One time, I found him lifting up the manhole covers and crawling down inside them. Another time, I was busily cleaning the house when I thought I heard a chainsaw that sounded like it was in close proximity to the house. Well, I was right. I looked out into the back yard to see where the noise was coming from, and there I saw Jeremiah, chainsaw in hand, up in the willow tree cutting off some of the branches. We ended up having to give the saw away to our friends, so it would be out of Jeremiah's reach for his and our safety. He was only about nine then. One Sunday morning, Roger left for church as was his normal routine: first because he had to be there early, and second, he didn't want to bother waiting for us. I got myself and the children dressed and ready to go and as we walked out to my car, I saw that all four of the tires were flat as pancakes. "Jeremiah," I yelled, "what did you do?" My voice stressed, and my mind was racing a mile a minute knowing I had to get going or we would be late. "Oh, I thought you could just drive to the gas station and fill them up," he said as he innocently stood there with a smile on his face.

Another time I was driving along with the kids in the car, and there suddenly began a downpour of rain. I quickly reached for the windshield wiper knob, and turned it on only to hear the wiper motor going. There were no windshield wipers at all! Here we were, about six blocks from home, trying to make out where the road was with zero visibility. Needless to say, I was grateful to reach our garage and furious at Jeremiah and the danger he put us in.

School was a major distraction for my creative son who thought it was a complete waste of time. He decided early on that he was above everything his teachers tried to teach him. He was bored to tears and figured out quite quickly in first grade, as he announced to me, that the teacher was trying to trick him by saying that two plus one was three and one plus two was also three.

Back then, attention deficit disorder was relatively new and rarely diagnosed. He was a classic case and refused to play by the rules. He would throw his papers, homework, and any other teacher-parent communication away before he got home. He had a brilliant mind that was never at rest. When he was about five or six, he rigged up a string mechanism that hung over his bed, threaded around the room, and attached to the lamp on the table, enabling him to turn it off and on from the comfort of his bed. He would constantly dismantle anything mechanical to see how it worked, and what's more, he would reassemble it! He was inquisitive and blessed with boundless energy, always thinking of his next project. The only time I could relax completely was when I knew he was sleeping. He was increasingly becoming more than a handful and because Roger was gone a lot, I was in charge to handle it all—including the discipline, which never worked on Jeremiah.

When he was four years old, it occurred to me that my dirty laundry wasn't where it normally was. I began to look for it and asked Jeremiah if he knew anything about it. "Oh, I did the laundry myself," he said. "How did you get the clothes into the machine and how did you turn it on?" "Oh, I just jumped up on top and put the clothes in there and turned it on," he quipped matter-of-factly. "How did you know how much soap to put in?" "I just watched you!" "Then where are the clean clothes Jeremiah?" I asked. "They're in the dryer." I figured out that he had just kept adding more and more clothes from the washer into the dryer with each load he washed. I stood there shaking my head and asking myself what kind of kid did that kind of stuff?

When my parents would ask us over for dinner they would preface their invite by saying, "Come for dinner, but you can't bring Jeremiah." They learned the hard way what he was capable of. He would disappear into the basement and fiddle with their furnace and water heater. God only knows what else he did that they never found out about.

I was always trying to figure out why he acted out the way he did and what I could do. I thought maybe he needed a change in his diet. He craved sugar and ate it by the spoonful when I wasn't looking. At Halloween, he consumed all his candy immediately even though I would put it away with the intention of only giving it to him in small increments. He would search incessantly until he found it and consumed every piece. I even read about a theory regarding red food dye being detrimental, so I read every label and removed it out of his diet, gravitating toward more natural foods. Nothing worked. One day, his first grade teacher sat in my living room and, out of exasperation, said as kindly as she could, "Mrs. Vann, I am very frustrated with Jeremiah. He is disruptive in class and no matter what I do to punish him, he doesn't seem to care. Quite frankly, I don't know what else to do." Quite honestly, I had no answer for her.

When he was about ten years old, he would disappear for hours. I assumed he was out in the neighborhood playing, but later found out that he would walk nearly a mile from home and steal returned bottles from Haskell's liquor store, and bring them to Byerly's to redeem them for cash. He then took the bus into Downtown Minneapolis to go to Schindler's bookstore and play games at the arcade. Then he would take the bus home without my knowledge. Again, what ten year old does that?

As I was passing through the living room one day, I happened to look out the front window and saw my car driving by. Unbeknownst to me, Jeremiah was driving the car around the block, and had been without my knowledge. I forbid him to ever do it again and thought he got the message until he was found out on the day he ran into the side of the garage. No amount of punishment deterred him.

Around the same time, he and a friend broke into an elementary school in our neighborhood and vandalized it. The police came, picked them up, and took them to jail. It was a mystery to them as to how the kids gained entrance. Of course, I got the phone call to come and get him, but I decided it might teach him a lesson if he stayed there as long as possible before I had to pick him up. Sadly, the police said I had to get him by six o'clock that evening which made my plan backfire. I was at my wit's end and, with no help from Roger, afraid about what the future held for Jeremiah.

As a result of his latest and most serious antic, we received paperwork a few weeks later summoning Roger and me to go downtown to the Juvenile Detention Center for a preliminary hearing. As soon as we were called in for the one-hour meeting, Roger excused himself and didn't show up until we were ready to leave. I was stunned and upset by his absence. Trying to be one step ahead of Jeremiah was exhausting, and I wasn't getting any support from his father. By this time, Roger had totally checked out regarding what should be done with Jeremiah. I suspected he was dealing with his own demons at the time. His attitude and demeanor was indicating that there was something wrong, but what that was, I didn't know.

I tried to encourage Roger to spend more time with Jeremiah and work on the father-son relationship. In order to pacify me, he would take him and, as I found out eventually, drop him off at the arcade, hand him $20, and disappear for hours on end. Later, Jeremiah told me he wondered when and if he was ever coming back to get him. My son was getting an education I was not aware of.

In the early 1980s, Jesus People Church had outgrown the building at 24th and Nicollet which precipitated our final move to the State Theater in downtown Minneapolis. This would be the beginning of the end as things changed. Thus far, the success of the church seemed effortless, but the problem was that with continued growth and finances flowing, it became easy for Roger to fall into lethargy and lose his focus. Waiting on God to provide became a thing of the past as the ministry flourished and took on a life of its own. Busyness replaced prayer and pride replaced humility. Someone once said to pastors as a warning; be careful of the three G's: Gold, Glory, and Gloria. Satan uses these temptations day in and day out to attack God's anointed and sabotage ministries. He also uses past sins to haunt Christians and pull them back through self-condemnation.

I remember reading in John Bevere's book, *Honor's Reward*, that to retain honor it is important to stay humble in spirit because everything we have has been given to us by God. God had warned Bevere that those who fall often do so during times of abundance, not the dry times. This is what happened to us. Regrettably the outcome was a disaster.

Unfortunately, Roger and the co-pastors didn't feel the need to be accountable to or submit to seasoned pastors or mentors who could guide them through the phenomenon of a church that exploded beyond their wisdom and experience. Most ministries experience slow, steady growth, and they were not held accountable to anyone but themselves and a board of elders who were handpicked by them. The Bible tells us that there is safety in the council of other wise and Godly men. Proverbs 24:6 (AMP) says, "For by wise council you can wage your war, and in an abundance of counselors there is victory and safety."

There were power struggles, selfish ambitions, and a feeling of entitlement that snuck in somewhere along the line. God was left behind, but the machine kept going. We all know of huge ministries and pastors who have fallen from grace as a result of Satan's tactics. In spite of the internal struggles of which the congregation in general was unaware of, people continued to get saved, delivered, and set free as God's Word was preached. The Bible says that His Word does not come back void and it didn't. He was faithful.

Roger was gaining notoriety in Christian circles and ministries, and he began getting invitations to share his testimony and speak in various churches across the country. He was invited to be on the PTL Club and had his own vision of launching a television program. Roger Vann Ministries was birthed, and Roger began to travel off and on. Eventually, God began to speak to him about holding crusades in Nigeria and the Philippines, so he took a team and sound equipment and headed great distances to carry the salvation message.

God's Spirit moved mightily and even he was astonished as he witnessed thousands responding to receive Jesus into their lives. Every time he gave an altar call, masses of people streamed forward down the aisles and filled every inch of space in front of the altar area: tears flowing, hands raised high. The first time that happened, Roger thought that maybe they didn't understand what the altar call was all about, so he reiterated the invitation, "Anyone who wants to accept Jesus into their heart come forward," he repeated. They continued coming as God's Spirit fell, and miracles and healings were happening. Even though there was a language barrier and interpreters had to be used, nothing quenched the message, the power of God, or the people's response to the Gospel. It was determined there were over four thousand in one service that accepted Jesus.

6

The Bottom Drops Out

Eventually, Roger was asked to leave Jesus People Church due to his lack of interest and inability to show up for appointments, meetings, or daily duties. He could never be found and no one, not even I, knew where he was. Of course, nothing was his fault; "they" were just plotting against him and trying to take over the ministry for themselves. He blamed everyone and everything, and subsequently decided he could start his own ministry; he didn't need them. There were a segment of people who followed us, not knowing the truth as to why he was asked to leave. Roger was a functioning addict.

We acquired an old church building on 31st and Park Avenue in Minneapolis. It was ironically located just across the street from where our ministry first began at the Park House, only now I was feeling that our demise was on the doorstep. The new church was named Peace Bible. Roger threw himself into every aspect of getting this ministry going, and God faithfully blessed as people started to come. I became hopeful that we were given a second chance. It was nothing like the past, however, but sustainable for a couple of years. Then old patterns began to manifest again as responsibilities were delegated to others. Roger became lethargic and focused on his vendetta and feelings of being misunderstood and unfairly judged by "those" people. He had never let go of what he perceived happened at Jesus People. His feelings of "not being accepted or good enough" returned. He continued to wallow in the past as he strived to achieve and recapture the exciting days of old.

One warm July day in 1985, while vacuum cleaning, I happened to spy a brown paper bag hidden from view and neatly tucked behind a cabinet in the porch. I pulled it out and began to inspect what it held. Its contents sent me reeling and our match-made-in-heaven marriage into the proverbial shredder. This was a major turning point in my life, and I would never be the same again. As I stood there totally stunned, I didn't want to believe what I held in my hands. This couldn't be happening, not to us, not to me. What had I done to bring this on? The sound of my heart pounded in my ears as I pulled out the stack of inked-up papers that read, *PAST DUE*, *SECOND...*, *THIRD...*, and *FINAL NOTICE*. I choked and found it hard to breathe. In one split second my life went from tranquility to chaos.

I began to page through all the notices. Then, I came upon a professionally typed letter from the mortgage company that informed us that we needed to vacate the property. Vacate the property? That meant we had to move! One's greatest fear of abandonment, homelessness, financial ruin, loneliness, and extreme lifestyle changes were what my life had become within five minutes. The home I had prayed for, enjoyed, and found so much security in for ten years was about to be jerked out from under me. *What about my family?* I thought. *What is going to happen to us?* The questions swirled uncontrollably in my mind. I was in such shock I couldn't think straight. I began to panic.

The receipts I pulled from the paper bag began to tell me a story. What I discovered was that Roger was driving within a fifty-mile radius of our house to visit doctors' offices, in order to con them into writing out drug prescriptions for him. The letterheads were from clinics, healthcare centers, and now-care medical centers along with numerous others I didn't recognize. Did I miss the obvious signs or was he just so good that he could keep his elaborate charade going undetected.

I pulled out an unopened letter from Golden Valley Bank where we had our personal checking account. I didn't want to open it up in fear of what other disastrous news it might hold. I stood motionless for a moment, just staring at the envelope. My mind racing, I started to break out in a sweat. My knees weakened; my stomach was churning. Roger had always controlled our money and I was kept in the dark. He never allowed me to pay bills or be involved with decision making regarding our finances. I was allowed to write checks for groceries and household expenses but nothing more.

The bank letter read, "Our records indicate that although your checking account has been open here only a brief time, we have already experienced overdrafts and returned checks." Attached to their letter were two copied checks, one written for $300 and the other for $50. I quickly got to a chair to sit down.

"Oh…God! No! This is not happening!"

Evidently, Roger was depositing his paychecks and then knowingly writing out checks for cash over and above what we had in our account. He had opened this new account because he said the bank got the old one messed up and I innocently believed his explanation. He needed the cash so that there wouldn't be a paper trail when he visited doctors' offices and pharmacies in his quest to obtain his drugs. I was beside myself; angry, upset, and nervous, but decided I had to confront him with what I had learned when he got home that day.

"God, help me, help me, do the right thing…to say the right words," I whispered under my breath to the only One who knew exactly what was happening.

I knew Roger was due to walk in the door at any moment, so I didn't have much time to prepare myself for the discussion that was about to ensue. A couple minutes later, I heard him pulling into the garage. He came through the door unsuspecting of what was about to transpire and the question I was going to ask him. As I hung on tightly to my emotions, I wondered what else he was hiding from me. My heart pounded as I struggled to keep my composure.

"What is this?" I asked, as I handed him the bag. He looked stunned, totally taken off guard, then retorted angrily, "Why are you always so paranoid? It's just a few bills. I'll take care of them." He turned on his heel and immediately retreated upstairs.

I knew this information had the potential of destroying our lives and everything we had worked for, yet he acted like it was no big deal. *What?* I heard myself screaming inside my head. *This is an awful mess AND you just lied to me.* Right then, I saw myself on the outside looking in as my whole world had just collapsed. I began experiencing something that didn't make sense to me, and I certainly wasn't equipped to handle.

My fight or flight instinct kicked in. One thing I did know was that I needed to calm down, keep it together, and try and figure out what I could do to help myself and our children. This became a monumental task as I felt an overwhelming cloud of doom hanging over my head. *My husband is a pastor*, I thought. Questions began to deluge my mind. *What was I going to tell our children? Where would we go? How would the congregation take this?* Then self-deprecation. *How could I have not known our bills weren't being paid? Why wasn't I paying more attention?* A growing list of insurmountable questions grew inside my head, and I didn't have an answer to any one of them.

In hindsight, it's easy to see that the warning signs were in plain sight all along, but on a day-to-day basis, I convinced myself to believe that they were nothing more than blips on my spiritual radar. "There is nothing you and I can't handle together if everyone would just stay out of it," he'd say to reassure me. Unfortunately, he succeeded. He convinced me to take him at his word and trust him, time and time again.

As Roger continued to preach thought-provoking messages that were anointed by God, all I could see was the impending doom of destruction right around the corner. Things were getting so uncomfortable at home and in our relationship that in order to keep the peace between us, "it" was swept under the rug and not up for discussion. Even though my instincts told me otherwise, I took a submissive position still hoping for things to turn around.

As I mentioned, a big part of what drew me to my husband in the first place was his heart for God. He ate, drank, and meditated on God's Word seven days a week. He was still a man grateful for what God had delivered him from. I recalled that Roger's old lifestyle had left him barely able to read or even communicate with people, and that he had lived a hard life on drugs. He had become what was called a "burn-out." Then God healed, restored, and blessed him above and beyond anything we could ask or think. I thought of how God healed him of cancer and in the infancy of our ministry, if we were low on milk or short on cash, we prayed and God met our every need; He always did. How did we get here, and how did we not acknowledge that if He helped us back then that He could help us now? When did we take the wrong fork in the road, and how could we get back?

When you love someone, you want the best for them. The protection instinct kicks in and you try to shield them, yourself, and the ministry from the criticism of others. Yet, the fact is there is nothing that can be done to change the outcome until the truth is revealed. God sees everything and cannot allow sin to prevail, especially in the church. Much of what my family endured could have been avoided if certain things had come to public knowledge. Secrecy is a powerful tool that Satan wields, telling us that hiding things will make everything fine, and that what people don't know won't hurt them. It's quite the opposite; light dispels darkness and heals.

Roger's addiction began to strengthen as his dependence on codeine escalated. I am reminded of the lyrics of a Christian song by the group Casting Crowns called "Slow Fade." It depicts the truth of what I witnessed in him.

Roger was slowly relinquishing his life, giving it over to a dark side. Towards the end, he needed a huge amount of support, but would never accept it as he insisted on keeping his problem hidden, like all addicts, thinking he could handle it on his own.

Satan effectively kept him contained and bound up in his addiction. Twice during our marriage, he agreed to seek treatment but never really gave it a fair chance, so it was a waste of time and accomplished nothing. The third time I tried to encourage him to go into a program, he laughed in my face. "You can't make me go if I don't want to," he told me. I watched him withdraw more and more to the point that he demanded that the children stay out of his way and banned them from the porch which he deemed, "his space." There he could wallow in his predicament and lick his wounds. He had little to no interaction with them.

In trying to force him to be accountable, I used every approach I could think of. I became angry, threatened to leave him, then became compliant; but nothing I did or said persuaded him to seek help. The last time we consulted with a counselor, I pleaded with him to go into treatment and I quoted the scripture. "Therefore to him that knoweth to do good and doeth it not, to him it is sin" James 4:17 (KJV). I thought for sure this would convince him; after all, he was a pastor. Surely he would listen to scripture, right? My pleading fell on deaf ears. By this time, I was emotionally and mentally exhausted. I had come to the end of myself and was beginning to feel as lost as he appeared to be.

When he was not using, he was the sweetest husband and the most loving father. But when he was using, his response time slowed significantly, and his ability to reason clearly was nominal at best. His mind was blank and he was numb. He pushed everyone away.

Eventually, he regularly began experiencing black-outs, and I saw the toll it was taking on him. At times, I heard panic in his voice as he was desperately going over and over in his mind trying to recall the events of the last two or three days of his life. As much as I wanted to help him, I was unable to say or do anything to convince him to give it up. He definitely wasn't willing to receive any suggestions from me. I felt helpless: standing on the sidelines, crying out to God from the depths of my broken heart, watching my husband slowly deteriorate. It's like witnessing a cancer patient slowly dying a little each day and not being able to help them. It tortured me!

He continued to minister to those who didn't know him as intimately as his own family. I desperately tried to believe him when he would get himself ready for the day and tell me that he was going out to do God's work. I wanted to buy it, hook, line, and sinker. I loved him and I loved God. I certainly didn't want to stand in God's way of whatever lesson He was trying to teach him. It's ironic, but he was able to keep up the pretense quite well when he had to.

I knew things had escalated when one morning I woke up and noticed Roger had the blankets pulled up over his head. That appeared strange to me so I asked, "Why do you have the covers over your head, can you breathe?" I nudged him and waited for him to answer. I became perplexed and persisted with my question.

He slowly began to tell me that he was awakened in the night by this insidious "thing" (he hesitated to say its name although he knew it was Satan) that stood at the foot of our bed staring at him. He began to describe the creature as black: blacker than any black he had ever seen or experienced before. The "presence" had a flowing cape with a shroud that was pulled over his head; Roger continued, "Its eyes were piercing red and they looked right through me." It was a cold, sinister presence that embodied the deepest hatred and evil ever encountered by mankind.

The experience was so frightening that Roger wasn't sure if he was dreaming, if it was a figment of his imagination, or if it was real. He was hoping it was only a nightmare, so he rubbed his eyes and looked around the room to see if our bedroom furniture was in place and the wall hangings were where they were supposed to be. Everything appeared normal except for that figure standing at the foot of our bed glaring fiercely at him. He said he was so scared he was paralyzed and forced into a position that enabled "it" to make direct eye contact with him.

No audible words were spoken, but by using some type of mind telepathy, Satan sneered and with a fiendish smirk and a snarl in his voice said, **"I am going to destroy you!"**

I'm certain at that moment, Lucifer was giddy at the thought of carrying out his diabolical plan to destroy Roger: the person who had at one time inflicted huge blows against the gates of hell as he preached God's Word. Roger was able to snatch thousands of lost souls out of Satan's hands and present them spotless to God, washed white as snow through the blood of His Son, Jesus.

Now, if his diabolical plan could be carried out, he would go before God's throne, thrust Roger up in His face, and lodge accusations against one of His redeemed. He would prove what a failure Roger was, and now it was his turn to have his way with him and claim him for all eternity!

At some point in time, Roger let down his guard and allowed a crack to open up in his armor. This allowed Satan, who was waiting in the wings, to take full advantage of his weakness. Subtle thoughts placed in his mind by Satan, the same thoughts he used on Eve and Jesus during their times of trial, began to take root and grow as Roger embraced the deceitful lies and glanced back into the past, longing for the "high" he once felt.

After he described this frightening experience to me in detail, I wanted to know why he didn't rebuke Satan knowing we have power in the name of Jesus, as mentioned in Luke 10:19: "I give unto you power to tread on serpents and scorpions, over all the power of the enemy" (KJV). Roger knew this by heart, and had used it many times in the past.

"No," he whispered, as if he didn't want to speak out loud in case the despicable being was still lurking around. Then I sensed he didn't want to discuss it any further.

Why didn't he take authority over it? I pondered. This was a crossroad in his life: an opportunity to change some things and ask God to forgive him. It was then God revealed the answer to my question. Roger was battling with his addiction and inwardly knew that his unrepentant sin and guilt left him powerless against the evil one, the destroyer, the one who was out to take his soul. The Bible says, "For we wrestle not against flesh and blood, but against principalities, against powers, against the rulers of the darkness of this world, against spiritual wickedness in high places" (Ephesians 6:12, KJV). Roger felt he had lost his relationship with God and didn't have the right to invoke His power anymore. Sadly, he had exchanged it for an addiction to codeine, which in turn created the wedge between him and God, giving Satan the authority to take control once again. He handed it all over on a silver platter without any resistance. All he would have had to do at that moment was to make the choice to repent, cry out to God, and take back his authority. God never walks away from us, we walk away from Him.

Life limped on and the process of deterioration continued as issues were not spoken of and pushed under the rug in denial. His life spiraled out of control and every day was a struggle to get through. I found myself wondering what was coming and when and how all this would end.

Call me crazy and ask, "What were you thinking?" but in my desperation to reclaim my husband and my marriage, I mistakenly made a decision that a lot of women do. I decided that if we had another baby, maybe it would draw him back to us. I was grasping at straws at the time and certainly wasn't thinking clearly. I did discuss the idea with Roger, of course, and he really didn't say yes or no. In hindsight, I believe the reason he didn't object was because he knew that having another child would be the distraction needed to keep me occupied and not focused on the elephant in the room. I wouldn't be pressuring him to pursue treatment. I had my tubes reversed, and shortly thereafter became pregnant with our daughter Hilary. Born in 1983, she was a beautiful, delicate little girl with a sweet, quiet spirit. I was overjoyed by this little person. Then, quite unplanned, we were blessed with a fourth child, Kailee, in 1985. Nothing changed for the better on the home front, except that I now had even more responsibility with four children and an uninvolved husband.

7

The Final Straw

ON OUR SIXTEENTH WEDDING ANNIVERSARY, my life took a nosedive. The thoughtful people from our congregation gave us a free weekend at the Embassy Suites Motel. We decided to invite another couple to meet us for dinner down in the restaurant. Before we even left for our relaxing respite, I threatened Roger, in no uncertain terms, that if he dared to use any drugs over the weekend it would be the last straw and I would leave him. He assured me that I was being foolish and that he wasn't using anything anyway and hadn't for some time. He said he was on the mend and I had nothing to worry about.

This was going to be a fun-filled weekend with just the two of us. I still had a gnawing feeling inside and a fleeting thought crossed my mind that he might not be telling me the truth. It wasn't anything specific about his behavior that caused me to feel uneasy, but

I had a hard time believing him in lieu of all the previous broken promises. I forced myself to put it out of my mind, hoped for the best, and set out to enjoy the weekend

We pulled up to the Embassy Suites Hotel. He let me out at the front door and I proceeded to the front desk where I waited for him to park the car. After we checked in, we were escorted to our room and handed the keys.

"Let's go down to the restaurant and look at the menu before our friends come," I said, hoping he wanted to do the same thing.

"No, I need to take a shower and get dressed before we eat. Why don't you go down and meet them. They should be here soon. I'll join you when I'm done."

I immediately felt a check in my spirit that if I left him, somehow something would go terribly wrong. I decided not to leave. Then the phone rang; our guests were downstairs by the front desk and said they would meet us in the restaurant. Roger was in the shower and my excitement got the better of me, so I left to go meet them.

We greeted and hugged each other and decided to go ahead and get a table. We made small talk and waited, and waited, and waited! The waitress delivered our menus and we put in our drink orders. We waited some more. Roger still hadn't come down. I was angry and embarrassed. This could not be happening! We finally ran out of topics to discuss, and I was at a loss for words. After forty-five minutes passed, I really started to get nervous. This was not a good sign. Ten more minutes passed. Panic set in, but I remained calm and nonchalant.

Then Roger made his appearance. He had showered, his hair was combed perfectly, his clothes matched, and he was totally high. He could hardly speak. His words were slurred, and he was difficult to understand. He was talking nonsensically and his sentences were disjointed. When I did catch what he was talking about, I couldn't believe my ears! Was he talking about drugs? He was! I was so humiliated at this point I was beside myself. The three of us politely ordered our meals, ate while listening to his embarrassing jibber jabber, and hoped to get through this as quickly as possible. Everyone except Roger was uncomfortable. Nobody wanted to order dessert; we only wanted to excuse ourselves and go our separate ways. Our evening ended the way it started—horribly.

We said good-bye to our friends. My thoughts were swirling, *What were they thinking? Would they tell anyone about this evening?* I knew they would be discussing what had just happened on their way home and the thought of it made me sick to my stomach. I wanted to crumble onto the floor and disappear. Sunday services were a day away. *I just can't do this anymore. I can't hide it or explain away his behavior. I cannot and will not make any more excuses.* Roger made it perfectly clear that he didn't want and was unwilling to take my suggestion to seek counseling and get his life on track, so the writing was on the wall. *I will not be embarrassed anymore. I cannot put myself through this. This has got to end.* The line was crossed and I was done.

"I don't know God," I prayed, "how the church or people will react to this, but I'm putting this mess in your hands right now. You said to, 'cast all my cares on you,' so believing in faith that your word is true, and that you care for me, I *will* put it in your hands. Please help me God to know what to do when we get back to our suite."

I was so disappointed and weary from experiencing yet more of the same old broken promises. I was also acutely aware of a heaviness deep within my heart that things that were about to transpire would change the course of my life forever. As we took the elevator up to the second floor, no words were spoken between us. Roger was oblivious and I was beyond upset. My mind was in a whirlwind, and as hard as I tried, I couldn't put much of anything into perspective. I was torn apart and ashamed of the thoughts that crossed my mind. I was actually thinking of... leaving my husband. A part of me still loved him and wanted to work things out. I wanted to see his ministry continue and keep our family intact. Plus, my marriage vows were very important to me and I didn't want us to be a statistic. But under the circumstances, our future looked hopeless.

A myriad of thoughts rushed in and out of my head all at the same time as confusion, fear, and panic raced through my body like an adrenaline rush. *Was I to blame for some reason?* I questioned myself. Then anger set in: anger at him for dragging me into something I didn't ask for and didn't want to be a part of. I was incensed and couldn't look at him. I was unwilling to rehash the events of the evening, so I quickly changed and got into bed, turning my back to him in hopes of giving him a clear message; I didn't want to talk. I had nothing to say. He fell asleep immediately: totally oblivious to what was going on in me and the devastation he had caused. I felt as though I was standing there observing the aftermath of my life after a tornado ravaged and destroyed everything I held sacred and dear.

"God what should I do?" I asked. Suddenly, I heard a still small voice.

"Get up and look in his socks, in the top drawer."

"OK."

I could hear his heavy breathing, so I knew he was asleep. Quietly, slowly, insides quivering, I slipped out of bed and moved over to the dresser. Funny, I didn't remember him putting his clothes into the dresser: Why would he? We were only going to be here one night. My things were still in the suitcase. *What if the dresser knob was loose?* I thought, *Or the drawer squeaks as I pull it out? He could wake up!* Holding my breath, I carefully reached for the knob.

Good, everything is tight. I sighed in relief. *Now to slide the drawer open. I better glance back to make sure he is still asleep and not watching me.* I knew from the past not to mess with his drugs. If he were to catch me, one more argument could escalate into my being the recipient of his rage. The mere size of his stature was intimidating. He outweighed me by more than a hundred and twenty pounds. *Success.* I got the drawer opened just enough so that I could stick my right hand in. I began to feel around and took a hold of something that felt like a bottle. When I grabbed it, I felt a lightning bolt go through me. I was afraid, my heart was pounding, and I began to sweat. I paused and before I looked to see what was in my hand, I again turned to make sure he hadn't been disturbed. *Good, he's still sleeping. Thank you, God.* My emotions were at their peak, and my heart felt as though it was pumping out of my chest.

Roger, I'm thinking to myself, *I am so mad at you for forcing me do this, and for putting our family and the church people through this. You make me feel like a criminal, sneaking around trying to catch you at your own game.* Tears started to well up in my eyes. *No!* I caught myself, *I can't be sniffling and blurry eyed now.* I took a deep breath, shut my eyes tightly, and stood motionless for a moment. When I felt more in control, I slowly, carefully pulled my right hand out of the drawer, rolled the sock cuff down, and looked at what I was holding. Now I was remembering all his empty promises: the begging and pleading for me to believe in him. They were all lies, and now any thread of hope I had hung on to was instantly dashed! I held the love of his life in the palm of my hand.

I loved you, but now I hate you for doing this! It's not about me or the kids is it? It's about you! You don't care about our future, our house, or the wonderful people of our church. I am standing here looking at codeine. This is what you are in love with, and I cannot compete with it. I'm sorry honey. I'm sorry to all the church people for what I am about to do, but I am going to blow your cover. This was the hardest decision I had to make. I knew this move would abruptly end everything we had worked towards for sixteen years. I would now have to begin a new journey, on my own, I had to!

I had to get out of that room and go somewhere, anywhere, but before I left, I decided to send Roger a clear message. I took his bottle of codeine and poured the whole sixteen ounces of poison down the drain, then quietly moved over to my suitcase. I carefully opened it, and removed my street clothes. I was ever so cautious not to do anything clumsy or make a noise that could impede my resolve. I wondered if he could he feel me moving about the room. If he did, would he suddenly sit up and yell, "What are you doing?" That image going through my head, spurred me on to quickly dress, throw my stuff in the suit case and flee. The next hurdle was to close the suitcase being careful not to click it too hard. But before I closed it, I quickly glanced around the room to take an assessment making sure I had everything I needed.

Oh no! Where are the keys to the car, and where is the car? I thought. I stepped back to the other side of the room, and without disturbing his jeans slipped my hand into the front pocket. *Here they are!* I wrapped my fingers around the keys tightly being extra careful that they didn't jingle against each other and make noise.

I grabbed my suitcase, and pushed a towel up against the door lock to muffle any clicking sound. With the keys firmly in my grasp, I carefully took a hold of the doorknob to our room. This could be another potential problem; motel room doors never shut quietly. The heavy closing mechanism makes a distinct sound when the door shuts. Will he jump up and come after me when I shut the door? *I'm so close, almost there, I need to keep going and take my chances.* I froze for just a second. *Go-o-o!*

I opened the door and stealthily slid through the least amount of space I could to make my escape. I held the handle on the outside of the door, and closed it as quietly as I could. OK, I was out and off to the elevator. I ran. Now I began to wonder if the desk clerk would stop or question me. After all, it was three o'clock on Saturday morning and I assumed they would think it rather strange that I had my suit case and was leaving at such an odd hour. I jumped on the elevator and pushed the button for ground level. Stupid elevator, it felt like it was moving at a snails' pace. *Come on, come on, can't you go any faster?*

I feared that if Roger discovered me missing, he would come after me and could possibly beat me down the stairs to stop me. My imagination was running wild. I was afraid he would come up behind me and grab me by the neck. He would be furious and would cause a horrible scene. My mind raced as the elevator was approaching the ground floor. I pleaded, *Oh God, help me find the car, I have no idea where it is.* As I stepped off the elevator, I looked through the lobby and out the glass front doors. *Oh no, it's raining. This can't be happening. God, show me where the car is!*

Again, I felt the Holy Spirit tell me that I should go to the right; he had parked it in the farthest corner on the side of the building. Sure enough, I spotted it over by the dumpster. As I ran for the car, struggling with my suitcase, I again had that overwhelming feeling that he was going to grab me. I couldn't get there fast enough! I was such a nervous wreck that when I got to the car door I was fumbling with the keys so badly, I couldn't get a hold of the driver's ignition key to open the door. *Hurry up, hurry up,* my thoughts screamed.

Finally I was able to locate the key and position it in the right direction so that I could unlock the door. I flung open the door, threw my suit case in, jumped into the driver's seat, and instantaneously locked the door. I cautiously looked around, scared to death I might see him standing there in the rain, demanding I open the door. But all was quiet. I didn't see any movement around the car, so I turned the key, backed out, and headed for the first exit I came to. It didn't matter what direction I was headed, I just needed to get away from that motel and the ugliness of everything that had happened. I needed to get to a safe place in order to contemplate what I was going to do next. I pulled off into a parking lot on the 494 frontage road to take a breath and pull myself together. The adrenaline rush I had experienced making my escape had taken a toll on me. I was shaking, crying, and praying all at the same time. I was thankful I had made it this far without incident.

I ended up at Roger's parents' house at 6 a.m. They were surprised to see me so early in the morning and didn't know I had been sitting in front of their house since 5 a.m. waiting for some lights to go on so I could knock on the door. I was dreading the fact that I had to open up to someone else, especially his parents, and tell them what had been going on with their son: the person they loved and the father of their grandchildren. My hope was that they could give me some hope, some answers, some direction to help me sort all of this out and not be too angry with their son in spite of his downfall. I was fearful, however, that they might suggest that I end our marriage even though I knew it was inevitable at this point. Those words would be hard for me to swallow. I desperately wanted to see a logical explanation for all this, but the writing was on the wall and too obvious to deny.

My nerves were frayed and I felt as though I was on auto pilot. I now had to struggle to get myself off of this emotional roller coaster Roger had put me on. This was not the life I had planned for myself and my children. Now everything had to be exposed and put on the table for the world to see. It was especially painful because Roger and I were so well known, not only in the local Christian community, but worldwide as well. Judgment would be swift and harsh.

When they opened the door to let me in, Rosemary's expression said it all. She knew I was in trouble.

"Does this have anything to do with Roger?" She calmly asked as she sat me down at her kitchen table, and turned to get me a cup of coffee. She sat directly across from me and asked, "Has he been using drugs?"

I hesitated because I still wasn't sure if I could really open my horrible can of worms to Roger's mother. But how was I going to explain my sitting in her kitchen at six in the morning if nothing was terribly wrong? These were by far the hardest words I've ever formed in my mouth and harder yet to let them go. I knew it would be devastating to them.

"You can't tell anyone. I don't know if he can turn this around and I don't want to hurt the church or my family, but I really don't know what to do and I don't want you to be hurt or disappointed," I sputtered. My frantic speech probably wasn't making a lot of sense. My thinking was so fragmented. I couldn't think anymore. I was so exhausted and tired.

Rosemary went on to say, "I knew it, just how he sounded on the phone with me the other day, and there have been times before that I questioned it. How long has this been going on?" I didn't want to say the words out loud. I knew this was the beginning of the end. I had just opened Pandora's Box, and now it wasn't going to go away!

"It was back in 1976, when we both had walking pneumonia," I explained. "We went to the doctor and he gave us antibiotics and codeine cough syrup so we could sleep at night, without keeping each other awake with our coughing. I questioned Roger if this would be safe for him because he'd had problems with drugs in the past."

"That was long ago, Jackie. I have a handle on it, and nothing is going to happen; everything will be alright," he reassured me.

"Rosemary, I believed him! I didn't realize anything was happening until just before Hilary was born." By this time I was sobbing. My heart was broken in a million pieces.

"I don't want you to go back to him, he needs help," she told me. "Now go upstairs and sleep for a while; you're exhausted and need to rest before you decide what you're going to do."

As I laid there with my thoughts, I tried to connect with my biblical principles and hold on to what I believed my whole married life. I longed for my husband to come back to the Lord and to change his behavior, but now I had come to fear the man who fathered my children. I tried desperately to sleep, but sleep evaded me. After a few hours of pondering what my next step should be, I got up and went downstairs. Rosemary and Hale didn't know what to do either. What could they say? It wasn't just my world anymore that was changing; theirs just took an unbelievable detour. This was my worst nightmare and theirs too. Disappointment and fear blanketed the three of us as we all grieved for what was to come.

My thoughts skipped to our beloved congregation. *How could I let this nasty secret out for all the church people to know? This is so humiliating! We're their leaders. We give instructions on how to live victorious Christian lives and we are supposed to be the example.* I didn't want anyone to know, not even family. Now everyone would know the ugly truth.

Every now and then, my mother-in-law would ask me point blank if Roger was using something, because she thought she had observed some strange behavior in him. Because I was scared and protective of my husband, kids, life, and church, I would cover it up and explain it away. I got used to it and I became part of the problem. I had hoped that one day he would come to his senses. Plus I felt a tremendous burden to not expose anything prematurely and be responsible for the fallout that would occur, knowing that it would destroy everything we had worked for. I had to protect the ministry and reputation of God more than anything. It had to be kept a secret, and I truly believed I could bring Roger around. If I just held out long enough, things would change for the better and this nightmare would be over. In retrospect, I built a fortress around myself and believed the lies of the enemy. Truthfully, freedom comes from exposure and God's reputation doesn't need protecting. I couldn't save anybody or anything. That was God's responsibility.

While Rosemary, Hale, and I were talking, I suddenly remembered that my sister Sandra attended a church that had a drug ministry. My heart leapt as a flicker of hope entered. I picked up the phone and called her number. They weren't home at the time but I still felt this might be the answer. Maybe they could help us discreetly get our lives back on track with the least amount of damage. Roger had tried to detox on his own a couple of times: once at home and another time, in April of 1986, at Woodstock New Life Treatment Center. Each time, it was short lived.

8

The Intervention

WHEN ROGER WAS RELIEVED OF HIS MINISTRY at Jesus People Church because of his inability to be dependable and involved, he felt persecuted and unjustly criticized. Never mind the fact that he wouldn't show up for meetings or appointments and was missing in action for most of the day.

This was typical addict paranoia and distorted thinking, but in his mind he was being persecuted for no reason at all. *Well*, he thought, *I'll show them, I'll start my own ministry. I can recreate another ministry just like Jesus People.* In reality, he was in no spiritual or physical shape to be starting anything. He was in denial and refused to acknowledge his need for a drastic change in his life. He forged ahead anyway thinking God blessed him before and He'd do it again. We founded a church on 31st and Park called "Peace Bible Church."

There were a segment of people who believed in Roger's ministry and followed us in the new endeavor. We did enjoy some success as God honored His Word. People were enthusiastic and committed, but it was a struggle to keep things afloat.

For three years, between 1983 and 1986, after I had discovered Roger's drug problem, we argued about his use of codeine. Now, I was finally at the end of my rope and I couldn't live with it anymore. I was growing paranoid under the pressure and at times thought I was losing my mind. The two older children were suffering through their own issues and began acting out more than what I could control by myself.

When I married Roger, I was filled with excitement and full of optimism for our future. My marital vows to God were for life. I cherished every word of our ceremony. I wanted to go through life and grow old with this man. What happened? Somehow I felt because I was abandoning my vows that I was a failure to God. My emotions were shredded. I finally concluded that if only one person is willing to work at a marriage and the other not, there is nothing that can be done to sustain it. I never stopped praying though because God is God and He can repair the most devastating of situations if an individual is willing. The key word is "willing."

As Roger's addiction worsened, my sense of security was totally non- existent. I tried to believe in the man I married but I asked myself if he was at a stage in his addiction that he would abandon his family. I was about to find out. Things were moving from odd to ominous. Roger came home late one afternoon and threw a book down on the table entitled *Crimes of Passion*. It was about how to commit the perfect murder. I was shocked. What was he saying to me? It was then that I began to fear for my life and the lives of my children. I knew at that point I needed to reach out to someone and do something quickly.

Here I was, sitting in my in-laws kitchen trying to make decisions about not only my future but the children's and Roger's too. I quickly made another phone call to Sandra and finally got through. I explained the events of the night before and told her that we needed help. She immediately contacted her pastor, Pastor Ona, and filled him in on the details. She asked him if he would get involved. Not much later, he called me and after a lengthy conversation, let me know that he was on board and would come alongside me to help resolve the devastating crisis I was in. He sensed the pain, anguish, and fear in my voice and got me in touch with a counselor/pastor that specialized in chemical abuse. Between the two of them, they were able to give me direction and instruction as to what to do next. Roger needed an intervention, now! There were many phone calls back and forth and a lot of hand holding. Thank God; they were my lifesavers!

The first order of business Pastor Ona and Pastor Schram told me I needed to do was to gather up his drugs. They suggested possible places he could hide them, and directed me as to where to look to find his stashes of codeine. It was so emotionally hard for me to go through all his things and I was convinced that if he ever caught me, I would be in physical danger. I collected four 12oz. and two 16oz. bottles over a two-week period and gave them to my sister for safe keeping until we could set a date for the intervention. Pastor Ona, along with a police officer friend of ours and I, did the intervention.

I was so nervous I was sick to my stomach in anticipation leading up to the intervention. I thought I would rather be anywhere else, doing anything else right then. I remembered vividly the birth of my fourth child upstairs, on our bedroom floor with a midwife, how I was struggling to deliver her. She was a large baby, and during the delivery it became critical that she make her appearance because she was going into distress. I was starting to become frantic and worried about the safety of the baby. Finally, it was over and we were both OK. As hard as that was, I would be willing to do it all over again instead of the intervention. I would even be willing to have all my teeth extracted without Novocaine (not that I did) instead of confronting the horrible ordeal ahead. I began questioning and second guessing myself. Was I betraying my husband and the church people we dearly loved? Would Roger explode into a rage? There was no going back now: no other option available, I told myself.

Pastor Ona instructed me to write down what I wanted to tell Roger and then at key points bring out a bottle of codeine and set it on the coffee table in front of him. We set the date. The morning we were to do this was sunny, warm, and the birds were singing. The doorbell rang. My stomach was queasy and in knots and my legs felt like Jell-O as I graciously opened the door and let Pastor Ona and our police officer friend in. They took a seat in the living room as I made my way up stairs to tell Roger we had company. I don't know if he heard it in my voice, but he immediately got suspicious and I think he knew something was going on. He always seemed to have a sixth sense. As I turned to go back downstairs, thinking he would follow, I heard the bedroom door close. I turned back around and tried to open the door but he had locked it. I went back down to where Pastor Ona was sitting and told him Roger had locked himself in our bedroom. Pastor Ona stood up, went up the stairs, and knocked on the door.

"Roger, open the door and come downstairs. I want to talk to you," he said in a calm but authoritative voice.

It took about ten minutes to convince him to come down. Pastor Ona continued to be very compassionate and nonthreatening. I was a bundle of nerves and with every cell of my being did not want to go through with this! But I realized we were now at a place where there was no turning back. I prayed silently. *Help me God; help me God.*

After Roger reluctantly sat down, I began my speech. It was hard to look at him. With each key point in my speech I finished with, "I love you. I don't want you to die. I want our marriage to be saved. We can work on this together." Then, I would put another bottle on the table. Tears flowed from my eyes and heart; I had never felt such pain and sorrow. At times, I had to pause just to compose myself; yet, the whole time I felt the Holy Spirit underpinning me every step of the way.

After I had finished what I had to say, Pastor Ona spoke with Roger about going into treatment. Roger said he didn't feel he could go because too many people knew that he had been a pastor of one the largest congregations in the Twin Cities, and he was embarrassed and humiliated. Pastor Ona let Roger know that he had procured a place for him at a facility in Pipestone, Minnesota. They had an opening, and he reassured him that while there he could be himself and not worry about other people.

"How am I going to get there?" Roger asked.

"Myself and one other person will take you and drop you off," Pastor Ona explained.

"When am I supposed to do this treatment program, and how long will it take?" Roger wanted to know.

"You will be there for two weeks, and then you will be evaluated and they will decide where you'll go from there," was the pastor's reply.

"Well, I have things to do," Roger said, trying to get out of it.

The excuses were presented, but Pastor Ona was persistent and unrelenting. Finally, Roger agreed to go. They packed his suitcase and were on their way. I knew all along he was angry with me, but I convinced myself that someday he would thank me. At least, that is what I hoped for.

It was a tremendous relief for me after it was all over. Little did I know, it was going to be short-lived. My counselor gave me her home phone and cell number and told me to call her every day or more if I needed to. My first day at home knowing he was in treatment was blissful! I felt a pervasive sense of relief and hope.

The next day, Pipestone Treatment Center called me late in the morning to let me know he had slipped away. They found out that he paid a farmer (with a bad check) to drive him back to the Twin Cities. He was on his way home! I was grateful they took the time to inform me, but as soon as I heard those words, I became flooded with terror. I immediately called the counselor to let her know.

"OK...take a deep breath Jackie, everything is going to be alright, we'll have a plan and all you need to do is to follow through with what I tell you. Can you do that?" she calmly asked me.

"Yes, I can," I told her.

She instructed me to back his car out of the garage, to put anything he would need for a couple days in the front seat, and lay the car keys under the front driver's mat.

"Go into the house and lock all the doors and windows. Do not open any doors unless you know for sure who it is," she said emphatically.

This is the part of the story where it begins to get foggy for me because I was so traumatized throughout the episode. I can't remember where my three older kids went, but I do know they were with someone I knew. I remember having only Kailee home with me. At the time, she was only was five months old.

I called my sister Lynda and her husband John, and my other sister Sandra and her husband Jack to come for supper. I felt fairly safe having other people around. They came, and we ate together and had a good time. Everyone tried to keep the conversation positive and light. At about 7:00 p.m. John announced that he and Lynda were leaving. I mildly protested as I really didn't want them to go. John assured me that he thought it would be alright and I probably had nothing to worry about.

"You think so John?" I asked in an unsure and frightened tone of voice.

John's famous last words were, "Oh ya!"

About a half hour after that, Sandra and Jack decided to go home. When they were on their way home and were only two blocks from my house, they were almost run off the road by a crazy driver!

"That's Roger!" Sandra told Jack. She immediately called 9-1-1. Suddenly, I heard pounding on my front door.

"Let me in!" Roger was screaming to me.

"No! Go get help," I yelled back, as Pam instructed me to do. While holding Kailee, I dialed 9-1-1. I could hear Roger throwing all his body weight against the front doors, trying to get in. They were thick double-paneled wooden doors, and I thought for sure I was safe. All of a sudden, I could see them bulging each time he shouldered them.

I was panic-stricken and sobbing uncontrollably. I was hardly able to speak intelligibly to the 9-1-1 operator to tell her that if they didn't get here **now**, I was going to be dead! She kept reassuring me that they were on their way, coming down the street with their lights off so they could catch him. Then, all the chaos stopped and it was quiet. The doorbell rang.

"It's the police!" they announced. I was so traumatized that didn't believe them. "Come to your front windows. You can see me." I looked out. It was the police. They instructed me to open the garage door. When I let them in, they saw me shaking, crying, and hardly able to talk. They asked me if I was alright. I couldn't answer them.

"He's not out there; do you know where he went?"

"No," shaking my head. Right then the phone rang.

"If it's Roger, ask him where he is," whispered Officer Nelson. I picked up the phone.

"Hello?"

"Why didn't you let me in?" Roger asked.

"Because you need help, and you can't live here anymore until you go get help. Where are you?"

"I'm down on Highway 55 at the gas station," Roger told me.

I covered the phone and very quietly let the police know where he was. Then I hung up on him. I didn't have anything else to say. I had said everything over the last two years and nothing ever changed. Officer Nelson radioed to another policeman and told him Roger's whereabouts. They stayed with me until he was apprehended. While we were waiting for the other patrolmen to call back, the policemen inspected the front doors.

"Lady we don't know how these doors held, look here." They showed me how twisted both the deadbolt and the plates on the door into which the pins fit were.

I called my brother-in-law Jack and asked him if he could replace the metal parts on the front doors to secure the house. It was quite the job. Both the doors had to be lifted off the frame at the same time because they were so mangled that we couldn't get them apart. He did the best he could to get the doors to lock until I could get someone to do the proper repairs. I still didn't feel safe after all that trauma, but as long as I knew Roger was off the street, I could relax somewhat.

The police called back and announced they had him and that he did not cooperate without incident. Roger had tried to grab a gun from one of the policemen and ended up being hit with a club in order to be subdued. He was taken to jail where he was to spend the night. I called John to let him know what happened and told him where Roger was. He went right over there to talk with him. Whenever I think about this particular part of the story, I can visualize the scene as John described it. He was sitting on the jailhouse floor outside of Roger's cell with his legs stretched out, feet touching the bars. A bed hung from chains from the ceiling and Roger had rolled up a blanket for a pillow. When he saw John, he jumped up and began to pace, ranting on and on about the police and the injustice he was experiencing. He looked like a caged animal. He was cussing loudly, his face contorted.

For years, even before Lynda married him, John had been Roger's right hand man: his best friend. John was with him helping to put things together for Roger as he traveled place to place, here in the United States and around the world in Africa. He had laughed with him and argued with him; they were buddies. Most importantly, he knew Roger's heart for God. John had gotten saved at Jesus People Church, and Roger had been his mentor in the Lord. It was ironic that the ministerial pass John used to get in to see him was signed by Roger! Now he was sitting there witnessing an unbelievable sight. He grieved for his friend, and couldn't believe what he was seeing and hearing. He began to weep silently. This was not the Roger he knew and experienced life with. John tried to reason with him.

"Roger, if you ever believed in what you have preached all these years, stop what you are doing, now." Twice he appealed to his common senses, but Roger chose not to hear what John had to say. He was caught up in his rage, the same rage he experienced as a younger man; a rage that was again controlling him.

Roger snarled and cussed at John, which cut even deeper into John's soul. Roger was unreasonable. After pleading with him for about twenty minutes with no results, the guard asked John to leave. He left that night crushed and fearful of what the future held for his friend. I never asked John to relive that dark night as I knew it was heart wrenching for him. I let it lay quietly in the past.

Roger was released the next day and went to a motel to stay. He called me, and I told him he couldn't come home until he went to treatment. He refused. The writing was on the wall. I had exhausted every possible way to salvage my marriage. Divorce loomed over our future. I knew I had to lay down my hope for my marriage to be healed, and embrace what God had for my future.

KJNP radio studio, Alaska, 1968

At KJNP, Alaska, 1968

On my bunk bed in Alaska, 1968

Our house on Park Avenue, 1970

Roger in our attic
on Park Avenue

Jesus People Church, first building, 1972

Roger preaching in Pine City,
MN, July 1972

Roger, 1972

Hale & Rosemary Vann, 1973

Roger at Jesus People Church, second building, July 1975

Our home being built, Fall of 1975

Suelee, 1980

Earl & Shirley Jones, 1980

Roger in his home study, 1982

With Kizzy, 1984

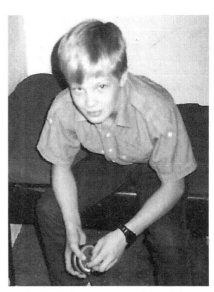

Jeremiah (13 years old) at the
Mississippi Home for Boys, 1986

Darcy, Kailee, Hilary and Roger at
his first treatment center, 1987

At Robbinsdale, MN Community Center, 1990

Restarting my education, 1992

Receiving my Associates Degree
from North Hennepin
Community College, 1994

Jeremiah and Darcy receiving USA
flag from Roger's coffin, Feb. 2000

Lynda, Sandra, and Jackie, 2007

Darcy, Jeremiah, Jackie, Hilary, Kailee, 2010

9

Someone Help, Please!

E ARLY ON, I HAD FAITH IN THE C HRISTIAN community—that it would come alongside those who are hurting and in need. I was to learn very shortly that wouldn't be the case with me.

I began making appointments with pastors throughout the Twin Cities who knew of Jesus People Church and Roger Vann. I hoped to get some temporary financial support so that I could take care of our immediate needs. I needed help with all the responsibility that was thrust upon me! After all, that's what the body of Christ was for, right? I became frantic as thoughts screamed in my head day and night. *What am I going to do? What about my kids? What do I do today, tomorrow, next week, next month? Where will we go? How do I get money, food, and shelter?* I had no answers, but I knew I had to do something.

Some of the pastors helped a little here and there but it didn't sustain us for any length of time. I felt like I was walking a plank and looking down into a bottomless abyss of dark angry waves ready to swallow us with each step I took. Loneliness became my constant companion. Sandra and I decided to call and make an appointment with a well-known pastor of a huge, local church to see if he would be willing to help us and give me some counsel. I proceeded to lay bare all the sordid details of Roger's addiction, losing our home, not having a job or finances coming in: basically the fact that we were destitute. After hearing our plight; he nonchalantly stood , put one foot up on a very expensive coffee table in his office, leaned over me with his elbow on his knee, and looking down at me (I was sitting on a couch) thrust his finger in my face and said; "If you don't reconcile with Roger, the devil is going to get you and your children!" He was totally devoid of compassion or understanding.

No matter what he said, I knew in my heart of hearts after all the years of trying to keep things together, and the devastation I had been through, that his advice bordered on evil. He had no mercy for me or my children. What I didn't know, but came to find out later, was that Roger had already talked with him and spun a story that I had left him for no reason at all. The pastor swallowed Roger's sob story hook, line, and sinker. Together, they formulated a plan to work together to pressure me into taking him back. I think this pastor thought he was going to be Roger's savior which would be a feather in his cap.

Don't get me wrong, I was grateful for anyone who tried to reach Roger and bring him back to what he was called to do, but I knew he wasn't willing to deal with the glaring issues and demons he struggled with. The well-wishers didn't know what they were dealing with. The thing Roger needed to do, and he knew it, was to humble himself, repent before God, and ask Him for complete restoration. But he was unwilling to do that. The thing he was willing to do was con people into thinking he was listening to them, convince them he had been dealt an unfair hand, and share that his wife was turning against him during his time of need. Evidently, there wasn't much discernment in those he duped.

It didn't take long before conflict began to arise between Roger and the people trying to help him. He began showing his true colors and refused to take their advice. His safety net was unraveling as he continued to walk his path of destruction. I believe at this time Roger's agenda was to use these people to try and convince me that I should accept what had happened and go back to life as usual without holding him accountable or requiring him to take ownership of his problems.

I was resolved. I couldn't do that, not for my children and not for me! After a tough week of having no food, and the kids and I being forced to eat popcorn for three days, I saw on the news that people were trying to figure out how to save three whales that were trapped by ice and couldn't get out to sea. They were so concerned for the lives of these whales that they were pouring thousands of dollars into supplies and food for them. They even wanted to hire pilots to airlift the whales back out to the safety of the ocean. It seemed like they were willing to spare no expense on these animals. It hit me like a ton of bricks; here I was, just trying to put food on my table to feed my children, and people were more concerned with whales. Somehow, the gravity of the story was more than I could process. I wasn't savvy to the ways of the welfare system or emergency services and had never been faced with not having food, shelter, transportation, or money before. I was a fish out of water and desperation was pressing in on all sides.

One day, deep in the doldrums of my despair, I happened to be at a local shopping center and ran into the wife of a pastor I knew very well. In fact, Roger and Dennis officiated at her marriage. They had originally gotten saved and served in various capacities at Jesus People Church and then, with our blessing, went out and launched their own, very successful church in Golden Valley. They were enjoying growth and wonderful success as God moved in their ministry. I was as surprised to see her as she was to see me.

At that moment, I wanted to pour out my broken heart to her and possibly receive compassion from someone I considered to be a woman of God. I was so desperate, I was grasping at straws, hoping for a kind word or a hug, which would've been like a cup of cold water in my dry and thirsty desert. My heart leapt, *maybe God sent you to pray with me, encourage me, give me a kind word.* I was certain this was a divine appointment and not just a chance encounter; surely He had led her there to minister His love to me. I definitely wasn't ready for what happened next. She reached out, gave me a quick pat on the back, said she would pray for me, and walked off.

I was stunned and disappointed beyond words. I felt like I had just been steamrollered. I stood there trying to get my bearings. *I don't believe this, what just happened?* I remembered back to when we were the pastors at Jesus People Church. Everyone wanted to be close to us and be our friends. Now, she was pacifying me with a few meaningless words that we all say at times and never follow through with. She seemed disinterested and anxious to be on her way. She had no idea of the enormous pain I was suffering or that she could have helped me tremendously by offering me a few kind words of encouragement instead of giving me the brush off. The pain cut deep into my psyche. I guess our relationship and past history meant nothing; love and humility had been replaced with insensitivity. I felt horribly lost in the sea of humanity. *Are there any Christians out there? Does anyone care? Can someone please help me?* It seemed that each day was filled with more and more disappointment and despondency.

I decided, in my desperation, that I would muster up my nerve and make some phone calls to churches in the area to ask for help. This went against every fiber of my being. I wasn't used to begging for help. Again, I received some help, just enough to eke out some food and immediate staples.

I needed direction in my chaotic world, and decided I could trust the leadership at Open Door Church. I made an appointment with Jeff VanVonderen. Jeff was an interventionist and an accredited psychologist. He listened intently as I poured out my heart to him. Some of the things I revealed concerning Roger's behavior was so despicable it was hard speaking the words out loud. I studied his every expression and body language, trying to get a clue as to what he might be thinking. He didn't appear to be surprised by some of the shocking things I had to say, but because of all the disappointments I was experiencing on a day-to-day basis, I had resigned myself to the fact that maybe this would be another dead end. If it was, I was ready to discontinue the session.

He exhibited such patience and kindness that I felt he was genuinely interested and concerned for me and our family. He enlightened me as to what was going on in Roger's world and confirmed what I was feeling regarding the future of our marriage and relationship. He laid my options out on the table and gave me Godly recommendations. Being an interventionist, he had firsthand knowledge of the mental state of an addict. I finally understood that I wasn't crazy and it wasn't my fault. I felt such relief and the spirit of peace flowed over me for the first time in a long time! I walked out of there that day with renewed hope. Even though I knew it was a baby step and far from over, I had a flicker of hope, just a flicker.

10

Moving Day

THINGS BEGAN HAPPENING SO FAST I couldn't keep it together. The house was in foreclosure and as word got around, the sharks began to circle.

Someone made phone calls and recruited a number of people to help me pack up the house. It felt wonderful to have a few friends rallying around me. They took it upon themselves to coordinate packers and arranged for people with cars and trucks to help with my move. This was no small task; this was a three-level house full of large furniture and everything we had accumulated over the years!

Just trying to get boxes and packing tape put me in overload. I couldn't sort out where to start first. Fortunately two of the women, Lynette and Patty, who had been making all the arrangements literally stepped in and took over. They noticed I was in no condition to make decisions regarding the packing. They began trying to locate a place for us to go when we were actually ready to move, which would be in two short days.

That night, I took the kids and stayed at Sandra's house. Because Roger was still sleeping at the house, I wouldn't stay there. Not knowing what his mental condition was, I was concerned how he would accept what I was doing. I wasn't sure if he realized that he would not be moving with us. At this point, my only concern was to secure a place for my children and me. He would have to live with the choices he had made and figure out where he was going to go on his own.

It was prearranged as to what time the moving crew would meet at our house the following morning. When I got there, I waited for other people to arrive before I went in. Upon their arrival, we went in and continued packing at a feverish pace. People brought in boxes and asked what they should put in them. It became surreal to me: watching friends and ladies from our church shove and cram all the stuff; what was left over of my life, into boxes and bags until the house was all cleaned out. What I couldn't take was sold off or given away.

At this point, all I wanted to do was crawl up in a fetal position, close my eyes, and cry out to God. *Where are you? Is this an awful dream or a cruel trick? Why couldn't I wake up and make it go away?* I never planned or wanted to end up as a divorce statistic but in my heart of hearts, I felt there was no other choice at this point.

To add insult to injury, that same day, I made the painful decision to put my beloved Doberman, Kizzy, to sleep because I knew I couldn't afford to feed or house her. My niece's husband Doug was kind enough to take the burden off my shoulders, knowing how much she meant to me, and offered to take her to the vet and put her down. I couldn't bear to think of the possibility of her ending up in an abusive home or being experimented on, so I opted to have her put to sleep. She loved car rides but thank God she didn't know this would be her last. My pain was unbearable. It wasn't enough to have my world blown to pieces and now I had to end my dog's life too.

Sorrow reached to the depths of my soul and tears rolled down my cheeks as if someone had turned a faucet on full blast. Memories of the enjoyment we shared during our running days, and the comfort she had given me all those years, came flooding back whether I wanted them or not! She was another innocent bystander that became a casualty as the result of someone's bad decisions. I struggled to accept that what I had to do was the right thing, but I had no choice. My anger against Roger grew as I blamed him for the state of our lives being annihilated and his disinterested attitude.

Roger, in his world of denial, stayed in bed while we were packing up all around him. He acted as if nothing was going on. *Bizarre.* Eventually, he did get up, took a shower, and left the house. A few hours later he walked in with a box of bakery rolls for everyone! Not only was I embarrassed, but totally bewildered. What is he doing? Then he disappeared for the remainder of the day. The next night was again spent at Sandra's. In the morning, we began to load up the truck. There was only one problem; I didn't know where we were going to go.

To my amazement, Roger wasn't at the house when we arrived to finish up. He eventually did show up, threw some of his clothes in his car and left. That was the day Roger would walk out of my life for good. I didn't know where he was going, he didn't say. As I kissed him goodbye before he drove away, I doubted that he really understood what he had done to us. I didn't know if he even cared. Shortly thereafter, my car was confiscated by a lawyer to whom Roger owed money and unbeknownst to me had given the title of the car to. He sent his secretary to pick up the car and return it to his office.

Drug addiction consumes its victims until all they think about is their need for it. The price they pay is exorbitantly high, but they don't care because they live in the moment. Roger had talked many times before about getting help, and I knew only time would tell if he would ever be well enough for us to be together again. Instinctively, I waved to him as I had so many times before, and watched the tail lights of his baby blue 1981 Cadillac, loaded with his few worldly possessions, disappear out of sight. At that moment, I thought of Satan's declaration to Roger: "I'm going to destroy you!" He had, and took the rest of us with him!

I wasn't aware of the fact that a longtime friend, a local pastor, had gotten wind of our predicament and began making plans to subsequently purchase our home, at a foreclosure price of course. I think he had an agenda when he found a house for rent and suggested we move in there. He baited the hook when he told me he would pay the first month's rent for us. I took it because it would give me some time to try and figure out my next step and clear my mind.

I was grateful to have a roof over our heads even though it was much smaller than the house we had just come from. The furniture I brought became a big problem. Roger always loved **big**, and when he bought furniture, it was big. I tried to stuff extra-long couches and tables into a living room half the size of the other living room. Unfortunately, more of my household items ended up in the garage instead of the house. It worked out though, because I didn't have a car to park in there anyway.

I was trying to make the best of it as I hung sheets over the sliding glass doors for some privacy. I thought they were pretty, and added some color to the off-white walls that were throughout the house. They were definitely better than nothing. My mom had decided to get some new curtains for her house, so she gave me her old ones for our dining area. Great! I felt like I was putting together a house for me and the kids, and the best part of it was that we were all under one roof. I started to feel somewhat secure.

We only lived in the townhouse on Ximines for two years. These were tumultuous days filled with confusion and fragmented emotions. Nothing was familiar except for our meager belongings, and the pressures of survival were always the white elephant in the room. I was so emotionally bankrupt myself that I didn't know how to help my broken children. We all struggled to certain degrees and every month would be nerve wracking as I contemplated how I was going to pay rent, buy food, and plan for our future.

Because I never had to work at a job since the day Roger and I married, I was completely inept at finding a job that could support us. I knew I probably would have to go back to school and get a degree of some sort, but I didn't know where to start. It was so overwhelming to think about because most days all I could do was get through one day at a time. I went days and weeks without laughing or smiling, and always felt like I was drowning. I sent out letters to local churches again asking them for help. Some of them were gracious enough to commit $50 or $100 a month for a period of so many months, which helped me pay my obligations and keep the utilities on. I had to obtain an attorney, which I couldn't afford, but fortunately he agreed to let me make payments of $10 a month until my legal obligations were met. It took me two years, but every penny was paid.

I desperately wanted to feel a part of the Christian community again, so I took the two youngest girls and headed out each Sunday morning to visit churches in our area. People were generally friendly and happy to let us know what their church had to offer as far as pro-grams and that was all fine and good, but I was looking for a place to belong, a safe harbor, a deeper connection. I always felt estranged from the body of Christians of which I was a part in the past. I never divulged who I was. I desired to be healed and wanted to be where God wanted me to be.

About a week after we had moved from our house into the townhouse, Jesus People's former accountant, Linda, called me. She reached out to us and offered to help with anything she could. I ap-preciated her more than she knew at the time. "Jackie, you need a vehicle to get the kids to and from appointments. If it's alright with you, I would like to sell the church's sound system and some other stuff to see if we can't get enough together to get you a down pay-ment to buy a second-hand car." At this point, Peace Bible Church was no longer in existence, and things had to be liquidated. I was ec-static that God had impressed her to think of me and so thankful for her assistance. I had just completed filling out all the paperwork to get us on the welfare rolls and the amount I would be getting didn't even begin to cover our needs. My rent was more than my check was going to be, but I knew God would provide and find a way for us so I was grateful for the smallest of help.

Linda became my guiding angel as she crunched the numbers and estimated approximately what I would need to put down on a car. She gave me $600. My sister Lynda knew a dealer who owned a car lot in Fridley, so we drove up there and looked at a car that would meet my needs. As I drove away, I thought how it was such a bless-ing that God provided for us. "Thank you God, little by little I am getting through this!" One step forward, one step back.

Life was so overwhelming I could barely lift my head off the pil-low every morning. My anxiety level was through the roof. We were all suffering the shock of our situation and the loss of the life we had known. The two oldest children began to rebel against school, me, and authority in general. I submitted to counseling appointments for Darcy, Jeremiah, and myself, but in spite of my heroic attempts, resolution evaded us and the problems escalated. Most of the time, I was busy making phone calls and trying to figure out how to make it each day. At the end of the day, I had nothing left to give the kids. I would emotionally check out or kick out and, quite honestly, my mind and body would go into numb mode. I was convinced that I must have been plucked out of my life and dropped into someone else's.

Roger had taken care of us all these years to the degree that I never had to even look at a price tag, or be concerned about the cost of groceries and if the bills were being paid. I had a nice car and never worried one second about our physical needs. I hated having to be on welfare with a passion, but I had no alternative at this point. I was completely ignorant of the welfare system, and didn't know how to navigate the nightmare of paperwork and phone calls necessary to obtain assistance. One day, I called on an old friend from high school, JoAnn, who had once found herself in a similar situation and she was able to help me navigate to where I needed to be.

I remember Darcy and Jeremiah being so embarrassed about having to use food stamps that they refused to come to the grocery store with me. In their minds (and I felt the same), food stamps identified us as poor and insignificant in the eyes of society. Darcy was very angry at our situation and had every right to be so. The world she had enjoyed for fourteen years had blown apart and catapulted her into an emotional tailspin almost overnight. As a young teenager, she didn't have the knowledge or wherewithal she needed to process everything and I didn't either. How could I expect it of her? We all had to work through what was dumped on us; we didn't ask for it.

Darcy went into a severe depression. She felt no self-worth; she was hopeless, isolated, and lonely. This then transitioned into a destructive pattern of running away and threatening suicide. She mourned for her home, her room, her security, and her friends. She had enjoyed the status of being the pastor's daughter and now found her life ripped from her. She too felt like her life had ended. One day, she took off and ended up at our old house asking to see her room again. My heart broke and I feared for her emotional wellbeing, so I quickly called the counselor that we had been working with.

Pam advised me to get help for her immediately and not to wait. I made some phone calls and ended up admitting her to the Golden Valley Health Center for evaluation. I remember vividly that it was late at night. I felt so helpless and awful bringing and leaving her with strange people in strange surroundings. It tore my heart out—what was left of it. They would not let me stay to comfort her. The staff said it was best that I say my good-byes and leave her alone to get settled. I felt so empty as I headed for home weeping uncontrollably. Thank you Roger, thank you devil for destroying me and my kids, I thought. I was hurt and angry. In spite of it, I immediately began to pray and felt God's ever-present peace come over me. His Word said He would never leave us or forsake us! I had to believe.

The next day Dr. Cochran M.D., two other counselors, a teacher, and I discussed the best treatment for Darcy. I wanted more than anything to help my daughter heal, to be successful, realize her dreams, and get through this. I would not allow our plight at the moment to dictate or define who she was. School was always a positive experience for her. She was brilliant and had great academic skills.

My two oldest children suffered terribly as a result of all that had transpired. Their wounds ran deep and it was hard for them to express the totality of their pain. In retrospect, I probably should have handled things differently but I didn't have the tools or skills to navigate these treacherous waters either.

It was suggested that Darcy have one-on-one counseling and group therapy. This would hopefully help her to sort it all out and move into a place of being positive regarding her future. They attempted to convince her that what she was experiencing was a bump in the road, and that her life didn't have to stop there. It was a struggle but she managed to pull herself out of a bad situation.

I was so proud of her in that she continued to work quite successfully within the support system put in place for her. She then went on to spend two years at Moorhead State College, transferred to the University of Minnesota, and graduated with a degree in Graphic Arts with honors. It was one of the proudest days of my life. She then became employed by the University where she was able to use her degree. There were good days and not so good days, but she was determined to transcend her circumstances and make the best life for herself.

Even though we can't escape its residual effects, we can minimize how negative things impact us on a daily basis. Life, in general, is a work in progress for everyone on the surface of this planet. Darcy went on to marry, have a family, and has become a wonderful mother and homemaker. She is a working mom managing a kitchen store, yet finding the time to be very active in her children's lives.

11

The Divorce

I MADE A DECISION TO GO THROUGH with the "D" word, something I never thought I would ever be a part of. After much introspection, prayer, and counseling, I knew in my heart it would be best for us all.

After I talked with two divorce lawyers who informed me that they couldn't work with me because they had already worked with Roger, I needed some divine direction. I began to pray and ask God to help me find the right person. I picked up the yellow pages and began to go down the line until I came upon Don Fraley in Wayzata. I felt strongly impressed to give him a call. It couldn't hurt. If this wasn't the one, he would say no, but I was convinced God wouldn't misguide me. Our first conversation was polite and cordial, and I appreciated that he asked me some tough questions as he tried to discern whether or not this marriage was reconcilable.

Don decided to accept my case and became a God-send to me. I felt somewhat relieved to be at this point. He was experienced and I knew he only wanted what was best for me and the kids. We weren't out to get Roger in any way. We didn't want to force his hand in case this whole mess could somehow, by some miracle, be turned around. That scenario was not to be, however, and our divorce was finalized March 7, 1989.

Even though I sensed God was with me, I still felt devastated, alone, angry, and lost. The few friends I had stepped back or out of my life as anger got the best of me and I lashed out at the ones closest to me. Satan is truly out to steal your dreams, kill your faith, and destroy your relationships. I was so totally destroyed and exhausted, I felt helpless to fight against his mental and physical attacks.

It became a chore to deal with my four children. My emotional pain felt like the size of the Grand Canyon, and a deep depression raged within me. It was relentless. Every waking moment it gripped my heart with the debilitating daily reminder of how alone I was. Every morning when I got up, I repeated to myself, "I don't want to live." I thought if I could die, I would escape the turmoil of the overwhelming decisions I had to make on a daily basis. It was unbelievably difficult to get through each day.

Then I began to think about the repercussions that would occur if I died and what my death would do to my children. Thankfully, I concluded that I couldn't be selfish enough to leave them to figure life out on their own. I would challenge myself. If I could just make it one more hour, four more hours, just until supper, then I could make it to the next day. It was horrible living like that. I hated waking up every morning knowing I had to go through this whole rotten repetitive cycle all over again. It felt like living in a bad dream that never ends. *When is my miracle going to come? Are you still there God?*

Am I going to make it? These were daily questions that wouldn't reveal any answers or relief.

My sister, Sandra, called every day to check in with me. She was the one who held me up when I felt I couldn't go on.

"Did you take a bath today?" She would ask me.

"No," I said. I had slowly become unable to function or even think through simple tasks. Taking a bath was overwhelming for me, so she gave me step-by-step instructions.

"Put Hilary and Kailee in front of the television, and turn a program on for them. Then go to the bathroom and run a tub full of water. Recheck the girls to make sure they are watching T.V., get into the tub, and when you're finished, call me."

"OK."

My dear, sweet older sister went through her own torture, and to this day, every time we discuss the past, I still see the pain on her face as she digs down to revive the memories of those dark and uncertain days. With tears flowing, she says "It was hard to be a bystander watching someone drowning and I couldn't swim." She was my angel, sent by God. Sandra and her husband Jack helped me keep my head above water and held my arms up moment by moment. She admonished me with, "You can do it; keep going."

Sandra constantly checked in with me. "Do you need food? How are the kids doing today? What's new? Are there any phone calls that you need to make?" She also seemed to know when there was a need and showed up with it! At times, my sister and her husband neglected to take care of their own obligations and let their bills go unpaid just so that we had food and shelter. Their love and protection was invaluable, and I will forever be grateful for their sacrifice!

A few weeks after we had moved into our townhouse in Plymouth, I became acutely aware that I was losing control of

Jeremiah. He was fourteen at the time and too much for me to handle. He was in dire need of an intervention. He was continually acting out at home and at school. His principal called me more than my
own family. But no matter what I did or said, he was detached and
unwilling to cooperate. We were advised to seek counseling, which
I lined up immediately. During these sessions, he was resistive and
unresponsive. He just plain wouldn't talk. The most we could get out
of him was a shrug of his shoulders. I was at a loss as to what was
going through his head, and things were escalating at home. This
forced me to take extreme measures for the protection of my two
small children and my son: another gut-wrenching decision I didn't
want to make!

In 1988, I found a boys' home in Mississippi that would take
him for one year. I had many conversations with the founder of the
home. I wanted to make sure he understood the hard place Jeremiah
was in. I asked so many questions, seeking to be reassured that my
releasing him to them was in his best interest. I really, really didn't
want to do this to my son, but I was at a loss as to how to reach him
and prayed that this would be a new beginning and breakthrough
for him. It cost $320.00 a month, and I had no clue as to how I was
going to be able to pay this. Again, I had to put my trust in God.

I knew I was going to miss him desperately, beyond words. He
was so special and had so much potential. He was my boy. I remembered him as a baby and the closeness we felt for one another, and
I looked forward to going through his growth spurts along with all
the other boy challenges. I never had a brother (I came from a family of four girls). Why did it have to come to this? I cried for days
knowing the clock was ticking toward the day I would have to let
him go. I felt like my heart had been put through a shredder and I
feared I would not be able to reassemble all the pieces. More anger

welled up inside me against Roger and our situation, and I didn't know where to put it.

Every day I got up, I had to keep going…somehow. Usually first thing in the morning, I grabbed my Bible and searched the scriptures for hope and inspiration and would feel refreshed. However, there were many mornings after doing my best to cling to God's promises, I paced back and forth in the living room weeping and wringing my hands, crying out, "Oh, God, I need you. Help me; give me strength to go on just one more day!" Sometimes my mind would become blank and I couldn't find any words to pray, but I knew God was holding me in His hands encouraging me to get up and face whatever the day held.

During the early part of my journey, one counselor asked me a question.

"Jackie, do you still believe in God?"

"Yes," came flying out of my mouth without even thinking about it. "Why?" I asked.

"Because people like you most likely lose hope and when hope is lost, suicide is usually the next step."

Even though I was going through a very dark and ominous valley, I knew God would be with me no matter what. I did the best I could with what I had to meet each challenge as they came, careening at me out of nowhere.

Bills and late notices were coming at me every day with threatening language. I had no money and no way of getting any, so bankruptcy became my only option. I remembered the commercial on TV that said, "This is all we do and we do it well." I made a phone call and a letter from bankruptcy court arrived one day with the scheduled date and time that I was to show up.

Even though I never owned a credit card, because I was married to Roger I was held liable as if they were mine. At one of my lowest points, not in my right-thinking mind, I actually entertained the idea of just giving up and going to jail. At least I would have free meals, a bed, and a roof over my head. I wouldn't have to worry about or organize anything. Decisions would be made for me! But once again, the awesome responsibility of being a parent jerked me back into reality.

I called my sister Lynda and asked her if she would accompany me to the court hearing. I was queasy and shaking, but she kept talking to me and telling me everything would be all right; it would be over shortly. I couldn't believe I was in bankruptcy court. On July 25, 1986, my mental health hanging on by a thread, the case went off smoothly, without a hitch. This seemed to be the first of all the bad things happening that I was pleased with—that is if one can be pleased with the ruination of one's future credit. But I felt a tremendous burden lifted off my shoulders, and for that I was grateful. It was one less thing on my plate.

My welfare check came once per month in the amount of $621. It shrunk to $521 after Jeremiah left for Mississippi. We needed food and rent, the kids needed clothes and shoes, and gas was a necessity along with car insurance.

I found a food shelf and thankfully got the food I needed. This was a huge relief for me: being able to put food on the table. It seems all my time literally was spent on the children and trying to keep a roof over their heads and food in their stomachs.

One day, I received a call from the pastor that was interested in buying our house in Plymouth. I felt somewhat comforted that someone I knew would buy and take care of the home we dearly loved and had held so many memories. We set a date to meet at my townhouse to sign papers. I called Linda, our former accountant, to see if she would be willing to be at the meeting because she was knowledgeable about those matters. She could advise me if there was something I shouldn't do. I felt I had an advocate and a safety net with her there should I need one. I knew that I wouldn't be receiving any funds out of the deal, but I had to sign off on the papers anyway.

To my surprise, the pastor and another man showed up early and began asking me questions I didn't know the answers too. I politely told them Linda would be arriving in a half hour or so and would advise me and answer their questions. The pastor went on to say they didn't have time and needed to get this paper signed...now! I hesitated because I was very unsure of myself and needed Linda's professional input to help me through this. At this point, I was feeling the pressure and was pretty shaken up. I sat down on my couch to wait for Linda when, without warning, tears started to flow as reality sunk in. I tried to maintain my composure but there was none of that left and I proceeded to fall apart in front of them.

They both excused themselves and walked in the direction of the front door. I was able to hear their conversation, and was appalled when I heard them making plans as to where they would go for lunch after this was over! I was devastated and deeply hurt by their lack of compassion and demeaning attitude while I was obviously having a hard time. To add insult to this whole fiasco, I had known this pastor and his family my whole life and mistakenly thought I could trust him to consider my family's welfare and not just his own greedy motives. I now felt victimized all over again. They turned, walked back towards me, and told me in no uncertain terms to sign the papers "now" or they would report me for accepting donations from people while I was on welfare.

Linda was trying her best to get to my house and would be there momentarily, but they pressured me mercilessly and it became too much for me, so I signed the papers under duress. As devastated as I was at that moment, I gave it up to God to deal with them. The Bible says that the Lord searches and knows the intent of the heart, and He therefore knew mine and theirs. As soon as they had accomplished their deed, they split in a hurry and were gone when Linda arrived. I felt bad that she had dropped everything and drove all the way from St. Paul for nothing.

12

Now What?

ONE DAY THERE CAME A KNOCK at my door. *Who could that be?* I opened the door to find a strange man standing there. He didn't look like a salesman or census taker so I greeted him:

"Yes?"

"Do you own a 1981 Cadillac?"

"No, but my husband does."

"Is it here?"

"No, why do you ask?"

"It's in repossession."

He looked at me with suspicion and acted like I was trying to hide something from him. He definitely didn't believe me when I stated that I had no knowledge as to where it was.

"Well, sir, do you want me to open the garage so you can see for yourself?"

"No, we already know you don't have it," he told me.

"But, here's our card. Will you let us know if you find out where it is?"

"Sure," I told him. I secretly hoped I would never see that car again, or Roger unless he had a miraculous visitation from God.

I closed the door and turned to walk away when there was another knock on the door. *Now, who could that be?* As I opened the door, there stood a man and woman, their arms full of folders that were stuffed with papers. They each had attaché cases. I quickly observed that they were both dressed in expensive suits and looked like well-manicured professionals. The man was short in stature and proceeded to do most of the talking. I sensed that whatever they came to see me about must have been pretty important, and because I probably wasn't going to get out of it anyway, I invited them to come in.

"Do you know why we're here?"

"No," *and I can't read your minds either.*

"Ma'am, you don't seem to be upset or concerned," said the woman.

Really? Really? I thought sarcastically.

I know they probably were taken aback by my reaction, or lack thereof, but considering everything I had been dealing with, I was unconcerned and nothing at this point would surprise me, assuming it had to do with Roger. Self-preservation for me and the kids kicked in, and I had no compassion or concern for him. He would have to fend for himself now no matter what the crisis.

I invited them to sit down at the table so they would have a place to spread out all their paperwork. They told me there was an investigation regarding Roger in process that required polygraph testing and lawyers. They asked me questions that I had no answers for. Roger and I hadn't had any verbal or physical contact for months because the divorce was still in process. This whole conversation confused me, and took me off guard. I didn't quite know what to think. It didn't take long for them to realize I couldn't be of any help to their investigation so they loaded up their stuff and left.

It seemed every other weekend was spent at "Now Care." Come Thursday or Friday, the crying would begin. It was such a routine that I never had to guess anymore; I knew what the problem was. One weekend, Hilary had an earache, the next weekend, it was Kailee. I swore there must've been something in the house that was making them sick. I wondered if there was mold in the walls or possibly some other toxic materials used in building the unit that they were reacting to. It was a mystery. It became an irritant to me as this was just another ongoing problem to deal with. It may have seemed like a small issue, but it did add one more thing to the pressure cooker I was already in.

We spent hours sitting in waiting rooms and yet nothing seemed to resolve their problems. I was relieved when the doctor finally suggested they get tubes in their ears. It seems that they had built up immunity to the antibiotics which no longer worked. Surgery seemed to do the trick for Hilary, but Kailee ended up needing to undergo it a second time which alleviated her ear issues once and for all.

With every day came the unbearable chore of trying to deal with a dysfunctional husband and emotionally fragmented children. Keeping a handle on my own sanity became a daily effort. I had to reason with myself. *It'll get better; you'll be OK!* My main and constant concern was always not far from my thoughts. How was I going to provide food and housing for my family? Added to that were other pressing things such as court ordered family counseling, appointments with lawyers and social workers, and ongoing medical appointments that put me on a perpetual roller coaster. Because of my limited resources, I had to ration food for fear we would run out before my next check would come. The children were very angry about the food restrictions and refused to adhere to the rules, so often times I would come home to find a week's worth of carefully planned food dwindled down to nothing. It would now only last a few days.

I soon became the "evil" parent for denying them food, their basic human right, along with trying to control the chaos that surrounded us. The natural inclination should be to close ranks, work together, and go into survival mode, but instead of us pulling together as a family, we blew apart. None of us knew what to do. As a mother who loved her children more than anything, I was determined to do the best I could to keep everything intact. All of this was so foreign to me. One minute I had a beautiful life with a home, car, food, money, health insurance, a husband, dog, and wonderful kids, and the next I was homeless with no car, no money, and little food. I had no job skills, and no future. In every direction I looked, the only thing I saw was a dead end!

I was barely hanging on when another curve ball was hurled at me. I received a notice in the mail that we would have to vacate the property by the first of August, 1988, because the town house was going into foreclosure. It seemed the landlord was taking my rent money but not paying the mortgage. Again, I would have to uproot my kids and was forced to pull up stakes.

Right before I received the notice, however, I had been starting to think and inquire about Section 8 housing, as it was getting increasingly impossible to keep my head above water financially. If I could get into government housing, it would afford me some relief for the present. I received a call that a unit had just become available not too far from where we were living, so I made an appointment and went on a walk through to see what the place looked like. I didn't want to be ungrateful, but while I was standing there looking around I thought to myself, *Is this, what my life has come to?*

This place was yet another step down from where I was living now. It was clean but felt impersonal and cold. The floors were covered with linoleum and the unit had no air conditioning. In Minnesota, summers can be unbearable when temperatures reach into the 80s and 90s and the humidity soars. There was a tiny storage area the size of a small closet located around the back of the building and no garage to store any furniture or household items which meant I would have to downsize even further. My biggest concern, however, was about the neighborhood.

I was very apprehensive as I observed the depressed neighborhood and immediately felt concerned that it was unsafe for me and the children. I was at a quandary. I desperately needed to find a place for us, but *oh God, was this it?* It wasn't pride that motivated any decision I would make because I certainly didn't feel I was above or entitled to better, but with each move it seemed as though my life and my identity was fading away. With each step I took, I lost more and more of me.

I was only given a few days to think about it and make up my mind. The agency explained to me that I would receive a phone call on Monday morning from them and at that time they needed my decision. I struggled back and forth all weekend, it was on my mind constantly; should I commit or let it go? I felt pressured with either decision. By the end of the weekend, I wished someone would just tell me what to do. The argument I had with myself came down to the fact that I didn't want to pass it up if this was God's provision for us, but neither did I want to be pushed into something that wasn't

His will. The wrong decision could very well be detrimental to us and that weighed heavily on me.

When the phone rang on Monday I was still considering the pros and cons and I was asking myself, *Is this the right thing to do, am I supposed to take this unit or should I believe God for something better*" Before I answered the phone, I quickly scanned the walls to see if God had written anything out for me, but no, there was nothing. No handwriting on the wall.

When I began asking a few questions about the storage area, the lady on the other end abruptly said, "Do you want the unit or not?" In my confused state of mind I remember asking her if someone else needed it more than I did. She simply told me "yes" and hung up on me. I panicked and tried, but was unable to reconnect with her. Now I felt I had just made a terrible mistake! I called my oldest sister Sandra crying, and confessed that I thought I had made an awful mistake by letting the unit go. I reiterated what I had said, "Did someone else need it more?" My sister Sandra said to me, "You said what?!" She and Jack were thinking this could have been a place for us to land temporarily and alleviate some of the financial burden, at least in our immediate future.

Looking back now, I see where God had a plan, and that my initial reaction, as stupid as I thought it was, was a part of it. At the time when I couldn't see two feet ahead of me, He was already working behind the scenes on my behalf. What I wasn't aware of at the time was that Sandra and her husband Jack had been casually looking for a townhome to purchase as investment property and had settled on a couple they were possibly interested in. All of a sudden, because of my predicament, it became a necessity for them to make a decision. They decided this would be an answer to my dilemma. They immediately put in a call to their realtor Mary, and pressed her into service to close the deal as quickly as possible and told her that time was of the essence.

Everything went into overdrive and only four weeks later, on August 1, I was able to take possession of a beautiful place that we would call home for the next seventeen years. I'm sure Sandra and Jack had many sleepless nights wondering if this was indeed God's will for them as well, but over time it turned out to be perfect for us all.

We were now in a safe neighborhood with a good school system and we were in close proximity to everything we needed. The kids were thrilled to have sidewalks on which to roller skate and ride their bikes. We spent lots of time outdoors and I was able to do the thing I loved most: gardening. The precious hours of planting and landscaping became my therapy and mental escape from all the trials that came our way.

There was a small wooded area behind the house that the girls played in and it had an abundance of wildlife to observe. This became our place of "normal." It was comforting and fulfilling and brought me back to a peaceful and tranquil environment. It was home! The hand of God and the plan of God for my life became a reality. How grateful I was. I couldn't praise Him enough, and for the first time in a long time I knew we would be OK. I could finally take a deep, cleansing breath now that our place of residence had become permanent and our basic needs were being met, yet inside, I was struggling emotionally.

13

Reality Strikes Hard

My troubles were far from over and each day, as I tried my best to keep things going in the right direction, the worse things seemed to become. I began having a tormenting dream night after night. It started in 1986 after Roger and I had gone our separate ways.

In the dream, I saw the vast universe. It was ominous, very large, and very black and I could only see a few dimly lit stars way off in the distance. In the middle of this universe, were two very large ropes, which hung down about two feet apart. I could see every detail down to the bristles sticking out everywhere on the beige hemp ropes. Then I saw hands, my hands, grasping on to them frantically and as hard as humanly possible. This terrified me because I instinctively knew that if I ever let go, I would be mentally lost forever, and forfeit my ability to find my way back!

Each time I had the dream, it became more vivid and frightening. Little by little, I began slipping further and further down the rope. I held on for dear life but no matter how hard I tried, I continued to slide. I saw large knots with straggly fringes at the very bottom that were about three inches long and below that, to my horror, nothing but vast darkness: no visible light, nothingness forever! I was about to lose my mind and was quickly sliding to the end of the only lifeline that was keeping me from falling into this never-ending darkness. Sometimes the thread we are held by is so dangerously thin, one more fateful tug and it could be over; I was literally hanging on to my sanity!

By this time in my dream, I was down to the knots at the bottom of the rope. My mental state was deteriorating quickly as I watched my fingers beginning to slip off the ends of the frayed rope. I was convinced that if I had the dream again, it might be the last time. I would be irretrievable forever and it was a good possibility that nobody would be able to bring me back to my right mind. It was horrible and beyond my ability to control, so I decided I needed help and put myself into counseling. When the battle becomes so intense and ongoing that we are in a weakened condition, reaching out for professional assistance is essential and nothing to be ashamed about.

I can't explain where this convoluted thinking was coming from but it was evident to me that the significance of the dream was that if I did drop off the end of the ropes, I would cease to exist mentally. I think that somewhere in my mind, I was still trying to be hopeful that Roger would come to his senses and rescue me, but at the same time I knew that the truth was the end of our marriage was on the horizon.

Anxiety attacks frequently plagued me. One day, I was driving south on Highway 169, when all of a sudden I couldn't remember where I was going or how to get back home! I began to panic and pulled over on to the shoulder of the road, stopped the car, and took some deep breaths. I closed my eyes to calm myself as I tried to regain my composure. As hard as I tried to pull information back as to where I was going, I couldn't think or even make sense of my surroundings. I was aware of cars passing by me but I didn't know where the highway was going and I didn't know where it would lead me if I turned around. So I just sat there for five minutes or so until my memory returned, thank God! I had never experienced anything like that before. It scared me to death that I couldn't control my thought process or reason effectively. I felt vulnerable and out of touch with reality.

I continued to also lose control of my emotions. It seemed that no matter where I was or how many people were around me, I cried and cried and cried. One morning as I was going to the bank and grocery store, I was determined to not cry in front of the bank tellers or the grocery store clerk. I repeated to myself over and over, *I AM NOT...I AM NOT going to cry.* But regardless of how hard I tried to keep my tears in check, inevitably, and without warning, something would well up in the pit of my stomach, move into my throat, and tears would gush down my cheeks. It was embarrassing and frightening as, again, it was uncontrollable. *What's happening to me?*

It became more and more difficult trying to think of excuses to tell people why I was upset to the point of tears and because this was happening so frequently, I began packing wads of Kleenex in my purse just in case the flood gates opened. Sometimes, when people asked if I was alright, I simply told them I was going through a divorce. But no matter how hard I tried to keep my emotions in check, I finally succumbed to the inevitable and just let it flow. I once wondered how my body could make so many tears. I comforted myself as I remembered a verse from the Bible that says,

> I am worn out from groaning. All night long I flood my couch with tears, drenching it with my tears. My eyes grow weak with sorrow; they fail because of all my foes. Away from me, all you who do evil for the Lord has heard my weeping. The Lord has heard my cry for mercy; the Lord accepts my prayers. (Psalm 6:6-9, NIV)

Early one morning, I received a phone call from someone from the welfare office who seemed inordinately happy that they got a hold of me. *What's going on?* I was thinking to myself. The worker was excited to give me some good news for once. Note: when you become a member of the welfare recipient club, people inject themselves into every part of your personal life. A social worker gets assigned to your case and shows up at your home on a regular basis. He or she helps to organize counseling appointments and set up programs for whatever the need may be in order to "keep you going forward." Their philosophy, I'm sure, is that if they can make sure at least one adult caretaker is functional and progressing positively, they would be less apt to have to remove the children from the home and put them into foster care. In other words, by caring for me they were investing in a more positive outcome for not only me but for the children too at less cost to the county.

When my social worker arrived, he proceeded to tell me that I needed to get out of the house one weekend per month for my mental health and wellbeing, all expenses paid. This would be on a monthly basis, and after a few months I would be reevaluated. They would even cover the cost of paying for a weekend babysitter and a motel room; all I had to do was pack some clothes and something to read. *Are you kidding me?* This was like someone handing me a pass to go on vacation to the Bahamas. I felt like I had hit the jackpot—pinch, pinch. To be able to have a couple days without worry would be such a healing or at least would allow me to be able catch my breath and regroup! I could spend time with the Lord and clear out the cobwebs before getting back into the daily battles of my life.

Once a month, the social worker would come to the house to observe, evaluate, and discuss what was going on with us. Our lives were all in perpetual turmoil. Darcy and Jeremiah were being monitored by the school system because of their constant truancy and I was frequently summoned to meet with teachers, counselors, etc. Darcy began running away and refusing to comply with any of the rules that had been established in our home and elsewhere by those in authority. They were both enrolled in specialized programs that were designed to help them move forward, but instead of taking advantage of them, they resisted vehemently and refused to take part. The worker that was assigned to evaluate their progress, or lack thereof, made suggestions to them, but his words fell on deaf ears. He became increasingly concerned that I would never get a handle on the volatility that was going on and worsening day by day.

In spite of what he observed, he was always kind and comforting and because of that, I remember clinging to his every word. Each time he visited, I hoped and prayed that he could provide me with a magic potion that would turn all this craziness around. After all, I thought, he's is a professional. He has the answers I need and I'm sure he has seen this kind of dysfunction all the time. Maybe he would throw me a lifeline before my Titanic sinks to the bottom. Not so!

Jeremiah did not move with us to the town home in Brooklyn Park. Two weeks after he returned from Mississippi, he began to act out again. Thus far, he had lived in Mississippi in a boys' home for a year, spent some time at St. Joseph's Children's Home, spent about a month at a teenage recovery center in Burnsville, was in foster care in Detroit Lakes (through a counseling group I was affiliated with) and, as a last ditch effort, spent almost a year at Holcomb House in St. Paul. One day, I received a call from Holcomb House and was told he could no longer stay there and that I needed to come and pick him up. I panicked. *What was I going to do now?* I had two little girls to protect and could not bring him back into the home. No matter how hard I tried to find help for him in the past, nothing worked.

I had exhausted every option, personal and professional, and paid out money I didn't have to try and pull him up and set him on the right path. Along with other teenage antics, Jeremiah refused to go to school, and was sniffing paint and glue. Finally, I came to the realization that I had no other option but to sign papers to give Roger legal custody of him. As much as I detested this decision, because I feared he would learn even more about self-destruction from his father, my back was up against the wall.

At this moment I had to "lay my Isaac down" and give him as a sacrifice to God. I had to trust that somehow he would survive and that God would never let him out of His hands. I saw him only a couple of times since that day and never dreamed over twenty years would go by before I would have any contact with my son. I guess Roger made an attempt to persuade him to stay in school, but I knew how strong-willed Jeremiah was and once he made up his mind to drop out, no one could convince him do anything he didn't want to do. The new living arrangements would be an eye-opener for both father and son because for the first time in both of their lives, they were in each other's lives. Neither one of them knew what that meant, but each would find out. Roger and Jeremiah were going to learn to sink or swim!

When Darcy was in high school, there was always turmoil between us. We were like oil and water and our personalities like sandpaper rubbing against each other. We both had deep-seeded issues to deal with, and I was at a loss as to how to help her. I made an entry into my diary on January 8, 1987. My heart's prayer for the two of us was, "The Lord gives his people strength. The Lord blesses them with peace" (Psalm 29:11, NLT). I longed for peace in our relationship, but it never came.

I never gave up praying and believing that someday we would enjoy one another and have a strong bond. I desperately hoped we could put all this behind us and live in harmony as mother and daughter. Jeremiah had required so much of my time and energy all the years she was growing up that I'm sure she felt pushed into the background.

To this day, I sympathize with her feelings of displacement and I validate her loss. She was always such a compliant and good daughter and, in her frustration, finally had enough of it all. Her counselor at the time placed her in foster care for a while and then took her into her own home to live with her. I was so grateful she had good people in her life to guide and direct her. I went to work cleaning "Chemical Free Ministries" building to be able to pay for Darcy's housing expenses. She flourished and began to re-engage and apply herself to her education. In no time, she was off to college and became able to live on her own for the first time. I was a proud and thankful mother.

We were now firmly settled into our town house on France Avenue in Brooklyn Park. Kailee was three years old and would be staying home with me, and Hilary would be starting kindergarten in a couple of weeks. I began to think about trying to further my education so that in the future I would be able to get a job that would pay me enough to enable me to support my family. The church life had been the totality of my life for so many years that I found it hard to switch gears and couldn't quite figure out how to function in the "real world." Roger was court ordered to pay child support of $238 per month, but I never received a penny. He was working a nominal job at a fire extinguisher company and I was left to figure it all out holding an empty bag.

I started making phone calls and somehow connected with the organization called "Wings" located in the Camden area of Minneapolis off of 42nd Avenue. They offered multiple resources for adults in transition. The staff immediately embraced me. This was my first baby step towards independence and it felt so good. The building was old and I remember walking up to the second floor on creaky wooden steps. Dark paneling covered the walls on each side of the staircase, and when I reached the top, the sun burst forth through the huge windows that over looked the street and freeway below. I felt exhilarated thinking *this is my new beginning* as I walked into the room we were to meet in.

Folding chairs were set up in a circle and it seemed that everyone in attendance was in similar situations as me. We all needed jobs and no one was sure how or what to do next. There were lots of handouts with tons of information given to each one of us. We then proceeded to go over each sheet. Upon conclusion, we were asked to go around the room to get to know each other by stating our name and what it was that brought us to this point. The group consisted of mostly women with a couple of men who were displaced as well. I felt such camaraderie with them.

This initial experience gave me just enough courage to think school might be possible; someday I could be a successful and productive wage earner! After a few weeks, I was put in touch with the Robbinsdale Adult Academic Program where I began taking classes and refresher courses. Just doing simple math again was a challenge. I was used to changing diapers, doing laundry, cleaning my house, or mowing the lawn. I'd been so far removed from school for so long that I felt like I was starting all over from scratch. In a way I was, only this time it seemed to come a little easier and faster for me.

One teacher in particular held a special place in my heart. I had never taken algebra before but she convinced me it was really easy. I wasn't quite sure if I should believe her and was very tentative until she slowly went over each step and... I got it; wow it made sense! Eventually, I successfully completed the program and was ready to move on to the real thing: college courses.

I was now directed to go to my old junior high school building, which had become the St. Louis Park Community Center. Located in this building was a plethora of agencies and information for displaced people such as myself. I found an organization called "Hired," run by a person named Nancy. She showed me exactly how to fill out the proper paperwork that I would need to enroll in community college. She walked me through the options available to me for financing such as Pell grants and other financial information to help me get started. I was so grateful and felt like I was finally on the right path.

14

The Next Step

I COULDN'T BELIEVE I WAS GOING BACK to school! School had never been my strongest attribute. In fact, I graduated from high school with Cs, Ds, Fs, and incompletes. I had to attend summer school in order to get my high school diploma. In retrospect, the reason behind my bad grades was not my lack of intelligence; it's that I was only interested in being with my friends and didn't apply myself to my studies. I was also planning to get married right out of high school and have babies, and my dad encouraged this line of thinking. So I didn't try and therefore didn't realize my potential.

Now there was a huge mountain in front of me and I was concerned, but I was also determined to get off welfare and knew this was the only way I could accomplish it. I sensed God was with me and believed He would help me get through the next phase of my life. I quoted the scripture, "If God be for me who can be against me… right?"

North Hennepin Community College, here I come! I registered for my general classes and met with a counselor who advised me of what classes I needed to take to get my associate's degree and be on my way to ultimately complete my education. I was excited and scared at the same time. As I began formulating a plan for my education that would ultimately get me into a profession that I could excel in, I decided to apply for jobs in professions I thought I might be interested in and subsequently took classes to support this endeavor. I gravitated towards and applied to the ultra sound program, but a year into my schooling found out they were accepting applications from "A" students, and out of those only five people would be selected per year. I was struggling to hang on to a "B" grade average in this class, so I wasn't even close to what was needed. I dropped out, disappointed that I had wasted a whole year only to find out I wouldn't be considered.

Then I looked into the dental hygienist program. The requirement was As in all the sciences or 3,000 hours of dental assisting. Well, I didn't have any of that so again I felt defeated.

Finally, I was qualified and able to apply for the registered nurse program. I was ecstatic the day I received the letter that informed me I had been accepted and instructed to report to the program's head nurse on campus.

I sat through orientation and after I received all the information, reality struck. I realized that in order to get into the nursing program, I would need to get child care because some of the classes were only offered during evening and/or weekend hours. As quickly as I felt a surge of hope, that hope quickly changed to despair when I realized I would have to politely decline the program because I didn't have anyone who could take care of my kids. Even if I was able to find someone willing to be there nights and weekends, I didn't have the funds to pay them. I racked my brains trying to think of someone in my family that might be able to step into that position. The problem was that everyone worked full-time jobs and the ones who didn't, my parents, were in Florida during the winter months. I couldn't believe after four grueling years of college education, I was stonewalled and unable to take the next step. I couldn't move forward because I didn't have child care. I was beyond devastated! It was at this time I decided to stay on welfare, although still considering a different direction with my education until something clicked. That way there wasn't any immediate pressure to find child care. As you know, you can't pull just anything out of the air. I learned a few years back when you don't know what to do, you don't do anything. There are times when it takes time for God to work and put the pieces together. I was just about to find this out.

In June of 1994, I proudly received my AA degree from North Hennepin Community College. My family and a few friends came to join in the celebration of my graduation. I don't know if any of them actually were aware of the fact that this was the very first time I had ever publicly graduated from anything! I was thrilled at my accomplishment. I remember being told constantly throughout the years by my father and husband that I was dumb and all I could do was take care of kids, cook, and clean! Yet here I was, diploma in hand—proof that I was smart.

While contemplating what I was going to do next, my wonderful niece, Angie, called and asked if I had ever considered going to school to be a surgical technologist. My immediate reply was, "No, doesn't it require a lot of education, like at least four more years of schooling?"

"No, just two," she said.

"I'd love to do that!" I said as a surge of new hope flooded my soul.

"OK, then I'll contact Rita at Anoka Tech and see if she can get you in."

Angie had connections there because that's where she had attended and received her degree as a surgical tech. After her graduation, she became employed at Oakdale OB/GYN and has been there for over seventeen years to date. God really used her to get me turned in the right direction and down the path that would eventually take me deeper into the medical field.

Phone calls were made and a few days later I received a call telling me that I had been accepted into the program and a spot was reserved for me! My spirit soared and I knew God was directing my every step. He was putting exactly what I needed in place. There were fifty-one people in our class: one of the largest classes the instructor, Rita, had ever taught. I was like a sponge absorbing everything I could about surgery and sterile techniques! I was elated about my future and excited to be learning. I studied for hours on end and worked very hard to get good grades. It paid off.

Labs were especially exciting as I learned how to wash my hands, glove and gown myself, and drape a dummy for surgery without contaminating the sterile field. I learned what type of suture is used on different layers of tissue, etc. Everything at that point was quite an accomplishment. As hyped as I was about every little thing, it was intense and overwhelming because of my age and the number of years I had been out of school. I was constantly overwhelmed with the volume of information we were expected to retain. Younger brains are like receptacles with retention skills; older ones are slower and resistant to retaining volumes of equations, biological and mathematical information, memorization of charts, etc. I hung in there and refused to be deterred no matter how hard it was. Finally, classroom instruction ended and I was ready for clinical training: where applying months of book knowledge became actual hands-on practical application.

The schedule for the clinical surgical tech program started at 7 a.m. and ran until 1 p.m. That meant I had to be up by 6:00 a.m., get myself ready, drive downtown, and be in the room and ready to go by 7:00. I needed additional income so while still in school, I applied for and landed a job as an orderly at Abbott Northwestern Hospital earning $9.58 an hour. My hours were from 3:00–11:00 p.m. Therefore, my days were over sixteen hours long including drive time.

Early on during this whole debacle called my life, my ultimate goal was to get off the welfare rolls as soon as I could. With my new job at Abbott, I was able to inform the welfare offices that I would no longer need their assistance. I was grateful and thanked them immensely for keeping us afloat when we were in dire need, but I must admit I felt a wonderful sense of accomplishment to be able to shoulder my own responsibilities. After I hung up the phone, Roger's demeaning words played like a record in my head, "you will never be able to get through school or make anything of yourself because you are dumb." On that very day, I was able to bury those negative words forever!

I was now in my mid-forties and the intensely long hours I had to endure everyday between school and work were becoming physically exhausting. I remember falling into bed fully clothed because I didn't have enough energy to even change into my pajamas. Sleep, when I could get it, was a premium for me. Every day, when I parked my car at work, I would sit there desperately wanting to close my eyes for a few minutes but couldn't because I was afraid if I did, I would go into a deep coma and possibly sleep through my shift. So I would relax for a minute or two then run inside to begin my evening shift.

I had no choice but to leave my two youngest girls, Hilary and Kailee, at home by themselves. They would call me at work all the time. It seems they were always fighting about something and expected me to step in to settle their inconsequential arguments. I felt pulled in every direction but knew that no matter what, I had to keep pushing through to complete my goals. I had the working-mother guilt big time and felt horrible for the girls, but subsisting on welfare was not what I wanted for my life or theirs. I thanked God every day that it was available for me when I needed it, but I resented having to be accountable to people who were just doing their job and didn't have a vested interest in me or my children. The long tedious hours and mental pressures of parenting, schooling, and working were exhaustive and taking a physical toll on me.

One day, I called my sister and completely fatigued and desperate I said,

"I'm at a cross road, the girls need someone home with them, I know that someone should be me, but in order to graduate I obviously need to finish school. I've come so far and am beginning to see the light at the end of the tunnel, yet I feel overwhelmed with guilt abandoning them for most of the day and night. I have to stay the course and finish what I started

"Sandra, should I quit school and go back on welfare so I can be at home with them, or should I forge ahead with what I need to do?" I asked.

Hilary and Kailee were now twelve and ten. They were technically old enough to stay home, do their homework, and complete assigned chores, but they were also old enough to get into trouble. I found out that Hilary was inviting her friends over, including boys, while I was gone. This was against the rules that I had established for them. Without adult supervision, it was a disaster waiting to happen, and although I was adamantly against it, I couldn't control it. I didn't want to sacrifice my children's health and wellbeing for my education. What alternative did I have?

"So, do I go back on welfare, or finish school?"

"Do you know anyone who could sublease? A single woman, a friend from the past or a school friend?" Sandra asked.

"No, I'm in my forties. How many single forty-year olds need a place to live?"

"What about Ernie?" she suggested.

Darcy and Ernie met at Concordia College in Moorhead, Minnesota. After they left college, they relocated back to the cities. Ernie was originally born and raised on the Crow reservation in Montana. He had a full head of black hair with loose curls and dark brown eyes. He stood 6'1" and could be described as a gentle giant. He could also be intimidating if he had a mind to be merely because of his stature. He was intelligent and a good communicator. He was patient, kind, and soft spoken, willing to listen and offer his opinion if asked.

When Ernie and Darcy's relationship split up, I totally lost track of his whereabouts. I knew he was working, but aside from that I had no idea where he ended up, or even if he would be open to helping me out.

Shortly after Ernie and Darcy returned to the cities, my first grandson, Conner, arrived. They lived in an apartment in close proximity to us. When Conner was about a year old, his mother and father separated. Darcy moved out, and Ernie moved out of our lives. Darcy and Ernie's relationship was somewhat like oil and water. Separate from one another, they were both awesome; together, they couldn't find common ground and subsequently decided to go their separate ways. Conner was everything to Ernie and he did try to stay in his life as much as he was allowed, but Conner has always lived with his mother and stepfather.

Regardless of the fact that his and Darcy's relationship was ultimately not to be, while they were together, he became a wonderful influence in Hilary and Kailee's lives. I too grew to love him as a son-in-law even though they never married. One time, during summer break, he took Kailee fishing on the Crow Reservation. She was introduced to a completely different way of life and experienced many interesting things. They, and some of Ernie's family, camped out in the wilderness. This was a first for Kailee—quite out of her comfort zone especially when she discovered she was surrounded by abundant wild life. She became too scared to sleep outside so Ernie made a bed for her in the car. To this day, the girls have fond memories of their adventures with Ernie.

When Sandra brought up Ernie's name, I did what I had done many times before, I prayed and put it on the shelf. "God, you know what is going on here and I'm not sure what to do, but I know you do, so I ask that if Ernie is to be a part of our lives again, please help me to find him, in Jesus' name. Amen." I wasn't quite prepared for my prayer to be answered so quickly. The very next day, as I was mowing the back yard, I looked up and there he stood!

"Ernie, I have a proposition for you. I need help. So, if you pay half the rent, look after the girls, mow the lawn, and shovel the snow in the winter, you can move in and have the whole downstairs to yourself. And," I added, "you'll get half the garage. What do you think?"

He was as happy as I was. We had a win-win situation. The very next day, Ernie arrived with his meager belongings and for the next seven years he enjoyed his own living space in the lower level of our town home. He eagerly took on his new responsibilities of two girls and a grown woman.

We had a lot in common; he loved being outdoors, gardening, and doing landscaping chores as much as I did. He was grateful to be with us, and we were grateful to have him. Ernie served as an authority figure anytime the girls wouldn't comply with household rules, which was desperately needed in our chaotic world. Many times he was called upon by me to confront issues in order to keep the household running relatively smoothly. He was always successful at keeping the lid on with his kind yet firm mannerisms. This is not to say they didn't challenge him, but they learned quickly that what Ernie said, went.

Ernie became our protector, and we felt safe having him around. He was often our sounding board when conflicts erupted. He was the peacemaker for us. When the girls had an argument, he was the one who calmly sat them down to discuss their feelings and hear their side of the story. He was fair but firm and always had their best interest at heart in his decision-making process. He was a strong support system for me as well. Sometimes I would come home from an unbelievably hard day of school and work totally exhausted and crying. He would sit up with me, no matter how late it was, to let me vent my frustrations and have my mini breakdown. Then he would calmly give me words of hope and encouragement that I would make it and everything would be OK.

Unfortunately, my arrangement with Ernie had a down side. Darcy was very unhappy that he was in my home and took it as a personal offense that I would allow him back into our family. Her anger over that resulted in my not being able to see my grandson for over ten years and I wasn't given access to her two youngest children although I longed to be a part of their lives. I now regret the pain it obviously caused her, and my pain went deeper than anyone could imagine! Over eight years later, I figured out the reason for our estrangement partly because we had never had a conversation about why she didn't want me in her life.

Ernie was a Godsend during those early years of me being a single mom trying to juggle school, work, and parenting. We have remained close to this very day. It gave me peace of mind knowing he was with Kailee and Hilary, making sure they were safe and had supervision while I was gone. They respected him then and still do. Ernie is now retired and is married to a wonderful woman from his home state where they are now residing. I keep in touch with him from time to time and I know Hilary and Kailee still call or text him when they need advice or help in solving a problem.

I felt I had all my important bases covered with Ernie living with us. I could get back to concentrating on school and work and was now rounding the corner and almost ready to graduate from the surgical technical program. I only had one more clinical to get through and I would be finished. It was so close, I could smell and taste the excitement of graduation and the beginning of better things in my life.

Unfortunately, the last clinical didn't go as well as planned. I arrived at the location, changed into scrubs, and got to my station early so that I could go over the material for the operation I was to be setting up for. The nurse in my room introduced herself and explained what pans of instruments I would need and where I would be standing in the surgical field. I proceeded to place the instruments on the mayo stand in the order the doctor would need them.

In order to graduate, the criteria are that all your sponges, needles, and blades must be counted before the surgery begins. As is normal procedure, I asked the nurse to count with me, but she kept getting interrupted by the doctor regarding the preparation and what he wanted done for his patient. The third time I asked to count, the doctor walked over to my mayo stand and took an uncounted sponge. Just then, my instructor walked in and observed this. She immediately announced that I had failed. The nurse tried to explain that she was in the middle of getting instructions from the doctor when he took it upon himself to remove a sponge from my mayo stand before she had a chance to count with me.

"Nope, she failed, and that's all there is to it!" She turned and was heading for the door, with the nurse following closely behind her arguing on my behalf.

"I couldn't get around to do the count with her, she asked me three times, we were just about ready to count when the doctor took that sponge off her mayo stand!" she pleaded. The instructor wouldn't consider changing her mind. It was done!

I was shocked and stunned by what had just happened. I choked back my tears. When the RN in the room looked at my face, she quickly got someone to step in for me before I burst into tears. This was such a fatal blow to me. I hurried as fast as I could to the nearest women's restroom, broke down, and started to sob uncontrollably. I was crying so hard that I failed to notice an elderly woman come in. She immediately saw how distressed I was and began trying to comfort me, putting her arms around me and telling me everything was going to be all right. She thought for sure someone in my family had died. I didn't tell her the real reason; it didn't matter and I couldn't speak anyway. All I wanted to do was get out of there and run for home. I was completely blindsided at what happened and couldn't believe I had failed the one last thing that was standing between me and the beginning of the rest of my life. To make matters worse, it wasn't even my fault. You know the saying about the light at the end of the tunnel? Well, that light was a huge train that just ran me over!

As crummy as I felt, now was the time to put it back into perspective. "God, you must have a reason for this. I don't know what it is but I am going to put my trust back in you," I was praying to myself. *I have come this far; I can't quit.* I was resolved, but that didn't stop the flood of tears that gushed out of my eyes. I left the bathroom on a mission to find another instructor from our school to get permission to go home. She could see I was beside myself and was very sympathetic towards me, even though she didn't know at that time what had just happened.

I made it home and proceeded to cry nonstop for the next three days. It was a major crossroad in my life. I was so discouraged at this point, my natural inclination was to just give up and accept my plight. On the other hand, I had invested a lot of time and effort, sleepless nights, and exhaustion and wasn't willing to succumb to this setback. I couldn't let my family down or myself for that matter. I dug deep inside, found my spiritual compass, and as soon as I felt I could function, I called the school to reschedule the semester I had just failed.

I pulled myself up by my bootstraps, renewed my determination, and jumped in with both feet continuing to work as an orderly and redoing that last clinical. The countdown to the day this would all end started over again. Back to sleeping with my clothes on and making sure I didn't fall asleep on the job. Back to juggling parenting, school, and job in an exhaustive state of being. Yet as each day ticked by, I knew I was closer to realizing my dream. This time everything came off without a hitch, and I passed the last clinical! I was finally on my way.

I received my diploma in the mail a semester behind my class, but I was thrilled that I had accomplished what I had set out to do. When I first started this journey, I approached college with fear and trepidation that maybe I wouldn't be able to handle college courses. It did take me longer to get the job done, but I did it! I was awarded my diploma as a certified surgical technologist on March 5, 1997. *I am not stupid and worthless.* I remembered what Roger and my dad had said in the past.

I now set my sights on getting a job in the field I had just graduated in. I began to send out my résumé to every hospital in the Twin Cities, and while waited for their response, I continued working at Abbott Northwestern Hospital for a few more months, then decided to quit as I was convinced that my wait wouldn't be long and soon I would get a phone call from one or more hospitals "begging" me to come and work for them.

To my complete disappointment, I began receiving response letters thanking me for my interest in their hospital, but informing me there were no openings for a surgical technologist at the time. As the weeks went by I became concerned, I desperately needed a full time job to be able to provide for my kids. I began to lose heart that I would ever find a good job and questioned God as to why I was having so much difficulty. I was becoming impatient and decided to take things into my own hands because God wasn't moving fast enough and lining up with my timetable.

I can't remember exactly how, but I became aware that the post office had some positions open. I had always heard that government jobs paid pretty well, so I decided to give it a shot. My preference of course was to find a job within the field I had worked so hard for, but at this point I was desperate and had to make a move. After all, I couldn't just sit around day after day waiting for the phone to ring with the perfect job. I called my friend Carol and asked her if she would be willing to take me to the main post office in downtown Minneapolis where they were taking the applications. I was somewhat intimidated about driving to unfamiliar places and, because she knew exactly where to go, she agreed to be my chauffer.

She then decided that as long as she was taking me, she may as well apply as she too had been on a job search. We both thought we would go in, fill out some paperwork, and be on our way; but after we were through with the applications, they tested us extensively to see how proficient we were regarding addresses, cross streets, numbers, etc. We waded through all that and left feeling hopeful that we had a good shot at landing something. Time painfully dragged on with no word either way.

A few months later, Carol received a letter telling her to come to the downtown office for an interview. She got a job and I was excited for her... but what about me? Two weeks later, I got a letter as well, asking me to come in for an interview; low and behold, on the very same day I listened to a message on my answering machine from Methodist Hospital asking me if I would be interested in a surgical tech job. *Are you kidding?* I could hardly believe my ears! God works in mysterious ways, and again He was right on time: His time. My prayer was answered and God was faithful. I excitedly called them back to set up my interview.

In the summer of 1997, I began my first job as a surgical tech and did so for the next seven years! I loved every moment of it, and my knowledge and experience grew daily. Although my wages were better, most of the time I barely squeaked by and it became such a source of frustration, I began to entertain the idea of going back to school to get my RN degree. As much as I detested the school idea, I knew I had no other choice. It seemed every time I got a raise, the cost of living would go up, and I could never get ahead.

I was still contemplating what I should do when one day at work, Fran, a nurse I worked with, commented, "This is the best job I've ever had." She was training in another nurse and was sitting in a chair outside the operating room so the new employee could do the circulating job by herself. I was aware that an RN's salaries and benefits were pretty good, and noticed that with her RN license she was able to afford all the basics in life that I was struggling with.

I finally had enough and grabbed the yellow pages. I called St. Catherine University and asked, "Do you accept older women into your program?" I was now almost fifty-one and felt time was quickly passing me by and my window of opportunity was probably about to close! The woman on the other end of the phone laughed and assured me it would be no problem. She said she would send me information about their nights and weekend program for Registered Nursing.

Déjà vu. I couldn't believe I was actually going back to school, but I knew that if I could achieve an RN degree, it would make our lives a lot more comfortable. Oh, I thought for a split second, if I could just meet a nice, rich man, he could become my "knight in shining armor," and would rescue me and I wouldn't have to endure what was ahead. Surely, that would be a lot easier than committing to three more years of school, which to me seemed like an eternity. No, I traveled that road before and it didn't work out too well for me so I decided to press on, convinced someday the carrot of financial relief would be my sweet reward.

Kailee was always nipping at my heels and crying the blues wondering why we were so poor and why she couldn't have what her friends had. I felt bad for my children and I knew they were having a hard time comprehending that in order to be able to get the things we want it would take hard work and patience. These episodes caused me to go back to blaming Roger for all the disappointments and hardship causing me to be the object of my children's anger and hostility.

I began my new quest in the fall of 2001. General classes once again had to be completed before I could even begin the nursing program. This curriculum was going to be much more difficult than what I experienced before. I made the decision to continue classes all year around so I could get the preliminary ones behind me as quickly as possible.

The actual nursing program began in the spring of 2002. With the mounting pressure of lectures, papers, quizzes, tests, labs, and off-site clinicals, I again began feeling like I was running out of steam. It was beyond difficult trying to deal with everything that was loaded on my plate. All I wanted to do was go home, go to bed, and take a Rip Van Winkle nap, rather than leave work, rush through the drive-thru to grab something to eat, and have just enough time to get to my clinical activities. I was working full time and juggling my schedule to coincide with school hours. Each time the new schedule for classes and clinicals would change, my supervisors at work accommodated and adjusted my hours accordingly. I couldn't have done it without their willingness to work with me!

Again, because of my heavy schedule, I agonized over the fact that I had hardly any time to spend with my two girls. I felt as though I was always on the outside looking in as they grew up overnight, or so it seemed. The pain of my absenteeism as a parent starting with Darcy and Jeremiah and now the two youngest was making me bitter and angry. I felt trapped trying to complete my education but didn't know what other alternative I had. I needed to have something or someone to blame; resentment against Roger continued to fester inside me like an old wound that would not heal. It was his fault that the last number of years had taken such a toll on me and the kids! I didn't know how to effectively process my anger, so I stuffed it deep inside and refused to acknowledge it or talk about it. There were no solutions in the immediate future anyway.

In retrospect, I should have dealt with my anger in a healthier way other than verbalizing my hatred for Roger in front of anyone within earshot. It was always there just lying beneath the surface and ready to explode at any time. Like a growing cancer, it ravished my peace and left me feeling alone and devastated. It was difficult, no, impossible to ever have anything positive to say about him. One day out of complete frustration, I proclaimed to my sister, "If *he's* in heaven, then I don't want to go there!" The thought of ever seeing him again drudged up all the deep-seated pain I experienced every day since our marriage fell apart. I just couldn't (or wouldn't) find it within me to be in a place of forgiveness; my wounds were still open and oozing! I was fully aware of the scripture that commands us to forgive others as God forgives us, and maybe someday I would, but not then. In some way, it made me feel better to vilify him, yet I knew the day would come, for my own wellbeing, that I would have to give all the ugly feelings to Jesus in order for me to be set free.

Because my life was so busy, I never had an opportunity to sit down, think things through, or seek counseling to help me clarify some things and get rid of my anger. It was easier to crucify Roger. He became my emotional dumping ground.

The following years, 2003 and 2004, continued to be a whirl-wind as I struggled to juggle life. There was no time for relaxation as it was critical that I pass every test with a 75 percent or better.

With each semester, the financial pressure of knowing that the longer it took for me to finish school, the further in debt I would become weighed heavily on my mind. It was like getting into a cab and watching the meter spin out of control while you're trying to get to your destination. I had to graduate as quickly as possible! All at once, I began thinking of the devastating scenario that played out just as I was finishing my last clinical for the surgical tech degree. Those awful words, "you failed," screamed in my mind. I cringed as all the horrifying feelings resurfaced in full force and hit me like a tsunami. *That will never happen to me again. I will make sure everything goes perfectly.* Because of that experience, I decided to fortify myself, just to be sure, by taking the Kaplan study course. The course would help refresh my memory for the boards after graduation. It covered everything from the very beginning of the nursing course all the way to the end, and I was determined to pass this test on my first try.

Also to solidify my preparedness, during my last semester I made sure that my nursing instructor and I were on the same page. I had many discussions with her making sure I was where I was supposed to be. I couldn't take any last-minute surprises. This was way too important! She and I had good rapport and she was very patient and reassuring when I doubted myself. I know at times I may have bugged her more than I should have, but she understood how vital it was to me that I have all my bases covered in order to be able to graduate on time. Each time before a clinical, I asked her how many points I had acquired and if there was anything I could do better.

"No, no…you're doing just fine, you're right where you're supposed to be," she would say to me.

One time, however, I narrowly avoided a disaster. I was assigned to a patient that was scheduled for surgery later in the morning. The patient was NPO (nothing by mouth). I made sure she was as comfortable as I could make her when it came time for my scheduled fifteen-minute break. The nurse that stepped in for me rushed me out of the room before I had a chance to tell her that the patient was NPO. I thought she was obviously experienced and would check the instructions on her chart or see the sign posted in her room that she was not to be given breakfast. Not so. The patient was fed and done eating by the time I reported back. My nursing instructor was very unhappy with me and let me know it.

Two weeks before graduation, two of my classmates and I were walking down the hall to go to the auditorium to have our graduation pictures taken. I was pulled aside into the office of my nursing instructor. Fear gripped my heart as she proceeded to tell me that I had failed because I was half a point short. *Half a point! What? No, please dear God, this cannot be happening again!* I was so dumbfounded I couldn't think. I had taken extreme precautions this time to make sure all my bases were covered so that I wouldn't have to go through the anguish I had experienced last time. I was trying to think of what I should do next. I was on the verge of panic. I was short of breath, my heart palpitating. I was in total shock and disbelief and was sure there was a conspiracy against me. *My friends are graduating and I'm not? They're having their pictures taken right now, and I'm supposed to be doing that too.*

Ok, I can't think; I can't think. This is not real. This is not happening again. No, I don't believe this! A half point short? There must be something I can do to fix this. She must have miscalculated and this is just a nightmare. Is this really happening? I couldn't get my head around those words. When I confronted her, she was annoyed that I was questioning her authority and unwilling to cut me any slack or even make a suggestion as to how I could make up the half point so that I could graduate. She wouldn't give me an answer as to why I was a half a point short. She said she added the points up and I was a half point short! End of discussion. I began telling myself to calm down and take some time to think everything through.

I went down with my classmates anyway to get our group graduation picture taken. I had at least earned that! It was almost impossible to smile for the photo, but I forced myself. I was on the verge of bursting out in tears after what I was just put through. Everyone around me was so excited, laughing, joking around, and feeling proud of their accomplishments; they knew their reward was coming in two weeks, their graduation certificate. Now what was I supposed to do?

I made an appointment with the nursing director at St. Catherine's to see if we could resolve the issue. Maybe then I would be cleared to graduate with my class this time. The news wasn't good, and once again I felt the depths of despair as I stood on the brink of a graduation that was denied me in the last hour. I was never allowed the privilege of knowing exactly what happened and, knowing nothing was going to change in my favor, I ate the sour grapes and registered to repeat the last semester. *God I trust you, I don't understand, but I know you're there.*

When the new semester started, my instructor and classmates were wonderful. I helped them out where I could, and I sailed through every clinical like a breeze. One day, my instructor pulled me off to the side away from everyone else.

"Jackie, can I ask you a personal question?"

"Sure, what do you want to know?" I said.

"Why were you failed last semester?" She inquisitively asked.

She seemed puzzled, and I was taken aback as to why she was asking me this. I guess I assumed instructors had access to pertinent information like this and that she would have known why.

"I was failed by half a point and had to repeat the medical surgical clinical," I stated.

"I know that, but why?" she questioned.

"I wasn't given a clear reason as to why. I even met with the director but was refused an explanation, so here I am."

"Well," she hesitated, "I am baffled by this. You do such a good job with your clients, are always helping out where you can, and show eagerness to assist your classmates with procedures they need help with."

Chidingly, I asked her, "So, you don't have any problems with me?" We both laughed and we went on our way. I never let anyone at my job find out that I had to repeat a semester. I kept it to myself, knowing someday I too would graduate. My joy returned, and I was happy I was getting close to putting all of this behind me.

I finished my last semester without any further complications and received my Associate of Science in Nursing in March 2004. I scheduled and took my boards right away, past on my first try, and received my nursing license April 29, 2004. Victory at last! I was unbelievably grateful that God was with me through all the disappointment I endured and kept me going even when I thought I couldn't continue. He was faithful every step of the way and taught me perseverance brings great reward.

Within four months, I was able to switch over from surgical technician to RN. I now circulate in the operating rooms and, on occasion, step back into the scrub tech job if need be. I love being in the operating room. It gives me great satisfaction to be able to work with wonderful doctors and co-workers.

15

The Lesson of Forgiveness

OVER THE YEARS IT HASN'T BEEN EASY, but I finally learned how to not allow my hurt and ill feelings to spill over to those I love. Forgiveness and repentance have become my two greatest allies. I found forgiveness. When we allow it and when it comes, it sets us free and propels us to go forward. Unforgiveness contains us and causes us to stagnate in a perpetual state of regression. It doesn't hurt the one we refuse to forgive, it hurts us. It was painful and, at times, uncomfortable, but I made a conscious decision to obey the scriptures and forgive with no strings attached—just like Jesus did when He gave up His life for me! He required nothing of me except to repent of my sins and to believe in Him.

I am committed to continue to put my trust in the Father who sent His Son so that I could be forgiven and be set free to live the best life God has planned for me. For years people have been telling me, "You need to write a book." I knew it was in me, but I didn't know when it would happen. I see clearly now that God first needed to do some more work within me.

As I mentioned, I had huge issues I was keeping to myself, and anger was one of them. I felt justified to hold on to those feelings that came as the result of events in my life that were thrust upon me through no fault of my own. Then God began to bring conviction.

The Holy Spirit brought to my attention my need to acknowledge that I was holding on to unforgiveness in my heart against my sister Lynda. I was angry at her for two things. First, she never phoned me. *Didn't she know or care about anything going on in my life?* Second, I was jealous of her having contact with my oldest daughter, Darcy. They both attended the same church and every time she saw Darcy, even though she knew of the estrangement between us, she would very innocently relay information about their conversation and things about my grandchildren. I didn't realize it at the time, but she thought it would make me feel better to get bits and pieces about what was going on with them; but I chose to take it as an offense. *If Darcy won't talk to me why is she talking to her?* My anger wasn't even rational at the time.

As God began to confront me about my attitude and unwillingness to forgive, I continued to stack the wall between us higher and higher, licking my wounds and justifying my reasons for feeling the way I did. I became the fault finder and I was convinced I found it in Lynda. *It's her fault, she doesn't call me. And why does she bother to tell me about her conversations with Darcy. How insensitive!* Lynda and I hadn't had much contact over the years as her life took her out of state for three years. When she returned to the cities, she and her husband were pioneering a new ministry. She was just living her life and, quite honestly, she wasn't aware of what I had gone through because I didn't involve her and I never bothered to pick up the phone to call her either. I was judging her for the same thing I was guilty of.

Because this is so dear to the heart of Jesus and is the key to unlocking and getting rid of old painful memories and re-establishing relationships with others and the Father, He continued to woo me toward offering forgiveness: not for her, but for me!

My oldest sister, Sandra, is a peacemaker, so she decided that the three of us should get together once a week. *What? Why would I want to get together with that insensitive other sister?* My initial reaction was "NO!", but to be kind to Sandra, I begrudgingly agreed to a weekly get-together. I decided that I wouldn't have to actually engage in conversation, I'd let Sandra do that; she's the talker. This, I reasoned, will only last a short time and then Sandra and I can go on with the way it used to be—her and me. I thought I had it all figured out, but God had different plans for our relationship.

The first time we met for breakfast, Sandra and Lynda were comfortable, conversed openly with each other, and had some meaningful discussions. The conversation soon turned to more spiritual issues, and Sandra was quick to respond with "Well," we need to pray about this!"

So, out came paper and pencil with which to jot down our prayer list. Each one of us had a family crisis of one type or another, so we decided that we would all pray for the same thing and just see what God would do. We even decided that we could minister to others in the community as God would lead and named our little band of prayer warriors "His Angels." In the beginning, we would meet for breakfast, share with each other what God was telling us, and speak to whoever He put in our path. Some amazing things happened as we obeyed the prompting of the Lord to minister to people through a word, a gift of money, or whatever we could do.

We soon realized that we really needed to spend more time in prayer and sharing in a non-public place, so we decided to meet in our homes, just the three of us. Lynda and Sandra were retired, so we only needed to work around my work schedule. On my day off (whatever day it was), we rotated to each other's homes for Bible reading, prayer requests, and sharing what God had done since we last met. We discussed what and how we should pray for our families and for requests from other people. The Bible states that: "Wherever two or three of you are gathered together in my name, there I am in the midst" (Matthew 18:20, KJV). We felt the power of that verse over and over as our prayers began to be answered one by one. Big things, little things, we prayed for them all.

Each time we met, however, I felt more and more ashamed of myself as God continued to convict me about my feelings against Lynda. Here she was, being kind and loving towards me, how could I continue feeling and thinking this way about her? About two months into meeting with them, I turned to Lynda and asked for her forgiveness. She had a shocked look on her face and had no idea what I was talking about. Tears fell as I explained why I had unforgiveness towards her, detailing how I thought she didn't care about me because she never called me when I was struggling through extreme hardships. She apologized for not being there, but that she didn't know most of what was going on. I felt so free and rid of that heavy weight I had been carrying for so long! The love of Jesus and His compassion permeated the room that day and since then the three of us have been closer than ever. Our three-fold cord will never be broken, and we are now able to present a united and powerful force against satan.

After that, I felt totally cleansed and thought I had gotten rid of all my anger. To my surprise, there was more to come. God continued to reveal some things to me that I had tucked away and hidden deep inside. He gently brought them to my mind for me to acknowledge so that I could repent and ask forgiveness from Him and others I had fought against. I wasn't the only one going through this process. In fact, each one of us—Sandra, Lynda, and I—began to search the innermost places of ourselves to allow God to cleanse us from anything that stood between us and Him. He would remind us of someone or something that had happened, perhaps in childhood or adulthood, that caused us to harbor ill feelings and encouraged us to give them up to Him. Just when we thought, *there, that must be the end of it. I can't think of one more person I need to forgive*, it never failed that something or someone would pop into mind and we would go through the procedure again. As a result, we felt closer to the Lord and experienced Him moving and answering our prayers in miraculous ways!

We began to pray for insurmountable, impossible things, or so we thought. One of the first things was that all four of my children would be back in my life. I had relationships with Kailee and Hilary, but our family wasn't complete until Jeremiah and Darcy were in the fold. As we brought our request before the Lord, Lynda saw in the Spirit, all my children starting their journey on the road back to me. We had no idea how or when God would answer this prayer but knew He would in His perfect time, so we just continued to thank Him and patiently wait.

God began to bring old friends back into my life from years past. One of those people was a woman named Denise. We made contact through Facebook and couldn't get on the phone fast enough to reconnect! Our initial friendship began in the Park House days and we were close friends for years. During our conversation, I was shocked when she mentioned how she felt that I had pushed her away and out of my life. I had no idea that I had shut myself off from friends and family. Evidently, I was so overwhelmed with my survival that I was oblivious to how I was acting and portraying myself.

It was also in that same week that my youngest daughter Kailee, while visiting me, brought up some issues between Darcy and myself. I opened my mouth in defense and immediately felt the Holy Spirit check me about my defensiveness. It registered with me that this was one of the things that was a roadblock to restoring my relationship with Darcy and her. I broke down right then and there at the kitchen sink and asked for Kailee's forgiveness. It was as if I saw for the first time what was really happening! I was guilty of displaying what I expected my kids not to do. It doesn't matter who is wrong or right. It doesn't matter who is suffering the most pain and who can justify their actions because of what they went through. We all have our story and perspective of what transpired and fighting to make people understand is futile. I needed to validate my children.

Out of my heart and eyes flowed tears of brokenness and shame as I asked God to set me free of this sin. He prompted me to write Darcy a letter to ask for her forgiveness and I wanted to forgive her unconditionally, just as God forgave me. I wanted to be her mother again and a grandmother to her children. I wanted to put the past behind because none of that mattered anymore! What did matter was that I needed our fractured relationship to be healed. I wanted that for all my children.

I was watching television one evening when something piqued my attention. The subject matter of the program dealt with how people respond to negative events that occur during their lives. For so many years, I carried the past like a fully-loaded backpack on my back. I wanted to be free from it but for some reason couldn't. The information I heard that night ministered to something deep within me.

The speaker began by saying, "The ability to bounce back or recover from adversity is not something we are born with or without. Even though resilient parents can serve as good role models, teaching us how to cope with adversity and how to adapt to life's challenges, we are still required as individuals to develop certain behaviors, beliefs, and actions that enable us to identify those difficult challenges and gain personal strength, wisdom, insight, and compassion by tapping into the 'power of hope.'"

She went on to say, "Resilience is not a new concept for scholars of the Bible in church history and Christians who have learned through personal experience. It can be a synonym for endurance and perseverance." The Apostle Paul writes in Romans 5:3-4, "…but we…rejoice in our sufferings, because we know that suffering produces perseverance (resilience), it will produce character."

In general terms, "Hope is the belief that no matter how painful life has become, it can be good again; no matter how great the betrayal, we can trust again. And this belief can enable us to pick up the pieces of our shattered dreams and broken hearts and decide what we can make out of them for the better."

We can believe and hope because of God's promises. "'For I know the thoughts and plans that I have for you,' says the Lord, 'thoughts and plans for welfare and peace and not for evil, to give you hope in your final outcome.'" And also, "We are assured and know that [God being a partner in their labor] all things work together and are [fitting into a plan] for good to and for those who love God and are called according to [His] design and purpose" (Jeremiah 29:11; Romans 8:28, AMP).

I posted the verse in Jeremiah 29:11 on my refrigerator, during those difficult years to remind myself that God was with me and, no matter what was going on around me, He wouldn't abandon me. He states in His Word that He never changes from generation to generation, and I knew that what He said He would do! My life has evolved as a testimony of God's grace and mercy extended towards me. His grace is shown when we get what we don't deserve, and His mercy is displayed when we don't get what we do deserve.

16

Road to Reconciliation

ALL FOUR OF MY CHILDREN, each individually unique, have dealt with the events of their young lives differently according to their perspectives. Darcy was initially angry and unforgiving towards me and blamed me for the failure of the marriage and inability to sustain our lifestyle. She was the most impressionable. At age fourteen, she was able to form her opinion as to why this all happened without the privilege of knowing the facts and without having the skills to make sense of it all. I never wanted to burden her, or any of my children, with the ugliness of reality.

I acknowledged to her that as I struggled to try and help her understand, I too was feeling abandoned and ill-equipped to keep body and soul together. I was unable to meet all her emotional needs. Her feelings of abandonment dug deep into her self-worth but I am proud to say she has superseded any expectations I had for her.

She is a wife, wonderful mother, and brilliantly talented woman. Our relationship is one-step-at-a-time and, with the help of God, I fully expect we will one day have a loving relationship, free from our past memories.

Jeremiah drifted aimlessly for over twenty-two years. From the beginning of his life, Jeremiah suffered complete disconnect in his relationship with Roger. This resulted in him acting out during his younger years and eventually gravitating toward self-medication and social noncompliance as an adult. He lived with Roger for a number of years, but not as a father figure guiding his son through life by helping him make good decisions for his future. They were more like roommates. Jeremiah too had God-given talents and gifts and a high propensity to accomplish success, yet never realized it because of his lack of focus or direction. Because he had no one to guide him, the only thing he achieved was how to survive with his street smarts, some of which he learned on his own and some was taught him by his dad.

For fourteen years, Jeremiah was the most difficult, frustrating child I had to deal with. He gave me no respite, just one problem after another which escalated each year. My biggest regret was to turn him over to his father, knowing he would have little to no guidance. I made a decision that day to "lay my Isaac down" on the altar of sacrifice—the hardest thing a mother can do. I didn't know what the future held for my son, but I knew Who held his future and that someday he would return to me. This little boy, who was a thorn in my flesh, has now become the biggest blessing in my life. I cannot thank God enough for watching over him and giving him back to me as a wonderful gift.

My relationships with my daughters are works in progress: one step forward and one step back, as this story continues to be written. Even though tentative at times, I believe God will continue to help us build our bridges. Sometimes things look bleak, but then my faith rises up and assures me that He who has begun a good work will be faithful to complete it. This biblical principal has become my personal promise as we navigate through our future as mother and daughters.

In August of 2009, Darcy and I cautiously began to text and talk on the phone. Shortly thereafter, I invited her family to come to my house for supper and a barbecue. The invitation was graciously accepted and we had a blessed time. My little grandson Joey asked if I was his grandma and could he call me that. "Yes, I'm your grandma and will be for the rest of your life!"

My heart was full with love and appreciation of what God had done. I was able to connect with my grandchildren and my daughter that I had been separated from for so long. It was surreal and felt a bit strange because of all the years of not being in contact. Over the years, Darcy and I had become two different people and would have to learn how to relate as mother and daughter again as adults.

As the years came and went (over twenty of them), I knew where three of my children were physically, but there was always one missing—Jeremiah. I often wondered if he was dead or alive. I would ask God, "Where is my son? Is he even alive, and if so, where is he?" As a mother, this really bothered me. I felt sad and concerned about him. I knew my heavenly Father knew where he was and what he was up to. I prayed for a sign: something, anything to let me know. Not long after that, I received a phone call. Actually, there were two I remember very distinctly. One was from a woman looking for Jeremiah for tax purposes. The conversation lasted for about forty-five minutes as we got sidetracked and ended up talking about our families, God, and wayward children. I really felt a connection with her, and maybe

God had a reason, other than her looking for Jeremiah, that I probably will never know.

The second call came at 1:30 in the morning and startled me out of a deep sleep. Usually I don't bother answering calls late at night or early in the morning because I always figured it probably was a wrong number or something bad that I didn't want to know about. But this time, without thinking I just got up and went into the kitchen to answer it.

"Hello?" I answered slowly and with great trepidation.

"Do you know a…Jeremiah Vann?" was the first question they'd asked.

"Yes, he's my son."

"Well, this is the sheriff's department. We found his driver's license at the State Fairgrounds and want to know where we should mail it." I was dumbfounded. *Why are you calling me at 1:30 in the morning to ask that?* It seemed fishy to me, and I wasn't coherent enough to put into perspective what he was telling me.

"Well, I haven't seen him in over twenty years, so it wouldn't do any good to mail it here to my address," I went on to explain to him.

"OK, thanks for your time, we'll hang on to it and figure out what to do with it." End of conversation.

I fell back asleep happy, confident, and thankful to God for the sign that my son was alive and somewhere in the area.

About a year later I was on Facebook when a box popped up from a person asking to be my friend. Sandra, Lynda, and I had been specifically praying for about six months for my two older children to find their way back into my life. The three of us had been meeting together one day a week for prayer and Bible study now for about a year and a half, continuing to petition God for whatever He laid on our hearts. This was the day that He showed Lynda that they were all on the road coming back to me, and that God was working on fully reconciling our family. What the devil had destroyed so many years ago was about to be restored and we were going to be a family again! All that evil, sorrow, and unforgiveness keeping our family fragmented no longer had power over us.

When I saw a request to befriend this person, and because I know God moves and works in miraculous ways, I wasn't completely surprised when I looked at the name in the box: Jeremiah Vann. For a split second though I thought, *Hmm, this must be someone else.* The profile picture was of a demon with a bloody spear, not my son. I then proceeded to look up the Jeremiah Vanns and found five with the same name but wrong nationality. I decided to take the risk to accept him as a friend. *Oh well, if this isn't my son, he won't want to be friends with me.* I looked at the clock and it was getting late, so I clicked off Facebook and retired for the night. The next day, I casually mentioned it to Lynda. She flipped out and was so excited.

"What did he say? Did you make contact with him?"

"I don't know if it was him, so I clicked to be his friend, then got off Facebook and went to bed."

"Have you checked Facebook to see if you got a response?"

"No, I haven't checked it today," I responded.

"Are you kidding me? Go check it and see if it's him and call me back!"

"OK."

I tried to not be too hopeful in case it wasn't him. I wanted to protect myself from any more disappointment. Before I clicked the "accept" button, I stopped to consider what repercussions this might have. Even though I longed for a relationship with my son, the actual possibility was somewhat frightening to me. I was going into uncharted territory and now wasn't sure about making this contact.

Was I opening Pandora's Box? I didn't know Jeremiah as a man; I knew nothing about him. I didn't know what path he had chosen to take in life. Then I wondered about how things would work out between him and his sisters, if it could or would happen. Would we all be able to come together as a family and work out our differences? I wasn't sure how to react to him. *Would he want to stay in a relationship with me, or me with him?* The questions and doubts permeated my thoughts. I began to talk to myself. *We have been praying and asking God to bring my son back into my life, right?* Obviously, if He brought him back, He would work out all the details associated with his return and whatever we needed to deal with; He would again complete the work He has begun.

Click.

Yes! It was *my* Jeremiah! He left the sweetest message: one that I had longed to hear for over twenty years!

"Hi Mom."

Just reading these words filled my heart with joy and anticipation. He had given his phone number and I couldn't dial it fast enough! "Jeremiah…" I don't remember my exact words, but I wanted to know where he was, where had he been for all these years, if he was married, if he had children, where he worked, and when could I see him? He graciously answered all my frantic questions as our new connection began.

The next day was Sunday. I arranged to pick him up for church and have him spend the day with me and my sisters. I quickly called and asked John and Lynda if they would be willing to drive me to his St. Paul apartment to get him. I was so excited that sleep evaded me for hours, but I didn't care. I was going to see my son, finally!

As we pulled up, my heart was pounding. There he was, standing in the front yard waiting for us. Jeremiah didn't look like the teenager I had last seen. I couldn't get out of the car fast enough. I ran to him and threw my arms around him, kissed his checks, and hugged him. Lynda heard me say, "My son, my son I love you!" We spent the whole day staring at him and hanging on to each word that he said as he answered question after question and we began to get to know him. I kept trying to see the little boy I remembered in years past. Now he had adult features that were unfamiliar to me, and I had to apologize for staring at him so much, but my motherly instincts were in overdrive trying to take in the sight and sound of my son's voice and his physical appearance.

Since that day, I pick him up quite frequently and bring him to my house and then deliver him back to his. Over the last number of months, our relationship has grown beyond my greatest expectations. He is sweet, kind, and considerate. He tells me he loves me and he is happy to have me in his life again. He calls and asks, "When can you come and get me? I want to spend time with you!" We laugh, talk, joke, and enjoy every minute together. He has had a lot of struggles during his lifetime but never lost that mustard seed of faith God puts in us all. Although his life was going nowhere and he was living the results of some bad decisions made over the last twenty-five years, he is now enrolled in school to further his education and is doing great at it. I am very proud of him and I verbalize that to him all the time. I believe with all my heart that all the years the cankerworm has stolen from Jeremiah, God will restore back to him. He is truly my miraculous answer to prayer.

My third child, Hilary and I have always had a special connection. Her personality has been—and still is—kind, sweet, and compassionate. She is still soft spoken and has been the cheerleader to her siblings, always ready to help. Hilary has been a second mom and mentor to Kailee as they both reside in St. Cloud. She has a wonderfully supportive husband, Nathan, who loves her deeply and always has her best interest at heart. She has her struggles as a result of the chaos we went through, but I am confident that she will emerge strong and healthy as God moves in her life. Hilary is a very gifted artist and when the time is right, her talent will bless others beyond what she can imagine.

Kailee, my most engaging and spontaneous child I will admit, has been a handful. She lives life to the fullest, flies by the seat of her pants, and sometimes rushes in where angels fear to tread. She is fiercely independent, but if channeled in the right direction, has a bright future ahead of her. I know she lacks the stability of a father figure and continues to search for that connection. My prayer is that God will provide her with the perfect man that can complete her, walk alongside of her and help her achieve all God has for her.

I had to believe that Jesus was with me, making my wrongs right, but I was a mess from all the upheaval that had been thrown at our family. I felt deeply rejected and perceived this as a personal attack from Roger. I needed the Holy Spirit to clean this mess out of my soul: clean out the thoughts, attitudes, and actions. The Psalmist David said, "He restoreth my soul" (KJV). The Holy Spirit teaches us and helps us. His job is to guide us into all truth. It's His job to help us not live deceived; He's our teacher. He doesn't show us everything at one time, but guides us and leads us into one truth and then into another truth and it keeps going. I needed to work with God to allow Him to help me work through my issues. He brings help and restoration (John 8:31-32). I needed to develop a knowledge of who I was in Christ, telling myself I am valued. I have worth. I have abilities. I can't do everything, but I can do something! I know God loves me. I know He's got a plan for me. I know I've got a future and a hope. I can just be OK with who I am.

Our past does not dictate our future, and because God has the master plan for each of us, we know this is not the end of the story. It will continue to evolve as He brings about reconciliation through our forgiveness one to another (as His Word commends us). We are challenged every day to forgive others as He has forgiven us with no strings or conditions attached. We anticipate our full emotional healing and restoration as we obey His Word.

I remained cautious as I counseled with various pastors, people, and friends during this life-changing ordeal. I learned that sometimes God uses people to speak to us. But, sometimes through His Holy Spirit or His Word, He speaks directly. This is witnessed by our spirit, so we need to ask God for the wisdom to know the difference, by asking ourselves, "Is this information I am receiving a word from God or is it just me?" Again as a safeguard, anytime we receive counsel it is important to measure it with the Word of God before it is received fully.

One of the most difficult feats I was confronted with was letting go of the past. Every time I allowed the memories to surface, I battled deep depression. It sucked the life and joy out of me, and getting back was at time next to impossible. The scripture I clung to was Philippians 4:8,9: "Finally brethren, whatsoever things are true, whatsoever things are honest, whatsoever things are just, whatsoever things are pure, whatsoever things are lovely, whatsoever things are of good report; if there be any virtue, if there be any praise, think on these things" (KJV).

2 Corinthians 10:5, "Casting down imaginations, and every high thing that exalteth itself against the knowledge of God, and bringing into captivity every thought to the obedience of Christ" (KJV).

I determined to walk in peace, sometimes it could be moment by moment in order to survive. I had to trade my fear for faith which sustained my sanity many times. You can never have enough faith to keep every problem away from you. Your faith is not to avoid problems it's to help you go through it! I gave God my brokenness and shattered dreams and He gave me His peace. "Peace I leave with you, my peace I give unto you: not as the world giveth, give I unto you. Let not your heart be troubled, neither let it be troubled, neither let it be afraid" (John 14:27, KJV).

Proverbs 23:7 (AMP) says, "For as he thinks in his heart (mind), so is he." This verse shows us that our thoughts are powerful, so we should make sure that what we are thinking about is what we want to become. If we put on the full armor of God, our minds will be protected from those thoughts that want to destroy us.

Every day, I am reminded that I only have today. I cannot obsess over the past, but I can confess God's love, omnipotence, omnipresence, and omniscience working in my life. He controls today, tomorrow, and forever and in that I am completely satisfied and content. All of mankind works tirelessly to be content. I am.

17

Where Are We Today?

When we finally come to the end of ourselves, God is patiently waiting. Roger had come to this point in his life. He was barely able to make a living, in poor health, and a shadow of the man he used to be. He was financially and physically destitute and cried out to Jesus, asking Him to please take him back. He had literally returned to the place he had been in his life those many years ago when he realized God was his only refuge. There was now no more pride, just brokenness and pain: pain knowing what he once enjoyed—closeness with God, a thriving ministry, and a wonderful family—was gone. The ultimate price he paid to chase his addiction. In the end, it left him empty and just trying to survive. These are the rewards one can expect to receive for serving Satan. In the beginning, sin seems so innocent and attractive. In the end, it is total destruction of body, soul, and spirit.

One day, he found himself on the doorstep of Minnesota Teen Challenge and begged Pastor Rich Sherber to allow him to stay at the facility. Rich graciously extended God's love and acceptance to Roger, and offered him a room by himself where he could find solitude and reflect on past years. He needed to find a place of forgiveness from God and he needed to forgive himself as part of his spiritual healing. Roger spent the next few months submerging himself in God's Word and in submission to Rich's leadership. His health continued to deteriorate and he became gravely ill. On February 27, 2000, Roger went home to be with his Lord and Savior—the One who never rejected or left his side even in the worst of conditions. His struggle was finished, and I picture him crawling up in God's lap where there is unconditional love and acceptance—the two things he searched for his entire life.

My sister Lynda decided to volunteer at Minnesota Teen Challenge to give something back for their kindness to Roger, and also because of the phenomenal success they have had in turning countless lives around. She made an appointment to talk to one of the staff and find out how she could volunteer for a period of time. She told me about her plans and, out of the blue, I said, "I think I'll come along with you." While we were sitting in Jim's office, Rich poked his head in the door to briefly say something to him when Jim introduced us. "This is Roger Vann's ex-wife." Rich stepped into the office and began to share Roger's story with us.

This was a divine appointment for me because up until that moment, I was completely unaware of what happened to Roger. I had struggled with total forgiveness toward my husband for years. This was the key that set me free. Now I am able to write this book. I never knew the suffering he had gone through; I just knew of mine and that of my children. I came to the realization that his suffering was even deeper than mine because he lived in a spiritual, self-inflicted desert bound in sin. I always wanted to punish him, but I now knew that it wasn't up to me to get even; it was up to God.

I have emerged a better person—happy and fulfilled. I am grateful to be a professional, able to enjoy the fruits of my labor, and take care of myself. I work every day in the operating room of a large hospital in the Twin Cities. I work with state of the art equipment in Gynecological (GYN), Urology, General, and Davinci (Robotic) surgeries. I work with brilliant doctors and staff that respect one another and work as a team for the well-being of all our patients. The reason these things are so important to me is because God has proven over and over that I am worthwhile. I am intelligent. I am loved. I am respected. The record that used to play in my mind, which was the opposite, has been silenced once and for all.

I enjoy the co-workers I am privileged to stand alongside on a day-by-day basis learning from and depending on each other as our day unfolds. No matter what happens and as hectic as things can get, we are a team—ready and willing to go the extra mile. I love sharing and praying for them if I'm asked, and consider my job a gift from God each and every day.

In 1 Corinthians, it states that God created us to live for Him, He's given us the gift of life and He wants us to live it abundantly. Personally, I find that my life can only be joyful and fulfilling if I have a close and personal relationship with Him. I am not satisfied to know about Him; I need to KNOW Him, who He is, what His attributes are, and what His promises are to me. There are no shortcuts to connecting with our amazing creator. More time spent praying and studying His Word will bring unbelievable results. He isn't a push-button, microwave God, and I don't recommend treating Him as such. I determine daily to relinquish my mind, body, and soul to

Him and trust Him to be in every decision I make and every part of my life: during the good times and the bad. He has extended to us an open invitation to seek Him and enjoy the blessings He has for us.

Problems give you the opportunity for God to be revealed! After all, how can you know God is a deliverer unless you've been a battle? How can you know God is a healer unless you've been sick? How can you know God is a provider unless you've experienced need? How do you know God is a friend unless you've experienced friendlessness? How can you know the fact that Jesus is the Prince of Peace if you've never had a day of trouble? How do you know God is a giant killer if you've never faced a giant? Our God is an awesome God! He is our problem solver and life giver.

He is the Potter (Who molds us) and we are the clay (Isaiah 64:8, KJV). Even though we have cracks and imperfections, we are the containers that God wants to fill with His goodness and light. It doesn't matter who we are, it matters who He is!

I remember being told by one pastor who counseled with me that I shouldn't look back into my past and only look forward. I agree. I no longer need to let my past dictate my future, but what I also realized is that it was important to reflect through those things and remember how God carried me every step of the way. He made me understand that what I went through made me much stronger not only in my faith but also facing the challenges of life in general. Most importantly, we can and must ask for God's help in absorbing the lessons He has for us as we walk through the fire.

As I look back, a few practices helped me to stay on the right path:

- I chose not to entertain criticism but rather think and say good things about myself instead. I did my best to admit my mistakes and confess my sins when the Holy Spirit showed them to me, but my focus was on my strengths and the good thoughts and plans God has for me—to give me a hope and a future (Jeremiah 29:11).

- I determined not to compare myself with others or how I thought things should be. Instead I tried to focus on Jesus and my relationship with Him. Meditating on the scriptures I've included at the end of the next chapter helped me to draw near to the Lord and receive strength and perspective from Him.

- Instead of being a victim, I pursued my potential through reading, going back to school, and focusing on moving forward, not living in regret. In the process I found activities that I enjoy and can do well, which I continue to this day.

In spite of how my dreams and aspirations for my own life turned out, I emerged a different, more mature and confident woman. And guess what—I like what I have become and really enjoy living life again.

No matter what your experience or story is, I can attest to the fact that the Father knows your sorrow and your plight in this life. But this is not our home. The rest of the story is yet to be written.

18

Restoring Hope and Finding Strength

Everyone has a paper bag. What does yours contain? Has its contents robbed you to the point of hopelessness, or has it made you stronger? Some of the things you may have extracted from your paper bag could be financial, relational, health issues, or spiritual desolation.

The first step to restoring hope is *acknowledging* there is Someone greater than us who has provided everything we need to cope with what we are forced to extract from our "paper bags." Whether it's catastrophic and life changing or just the daily struggles that get tedious and overwhelming, we have within our grasp the ability to ask for and receive comfort, direction, and healing from our gracious Heavenly Father.

The second step is *accepting* the "gift," Jesus Christ, God the Father's only begotten Son who laid down His life for our sins so that we could be reconciled to the Father and partakers of all the benefits and promises in His Holy Word. Titus 1:2 describes this life as "a faith and knowledge resting on the hope of eternal life which God, Who does not lie, promised before the beginning of time" (NIV).

So not only does that relationship, extended to all mankind, assure us of eternity in heaven but also helps us in our daily journey and sustains our hope.

Below are specific scriptures that gave me strength as I was going through what I have written in this book. Reading and meditating upon these truths from the Bible helped me to extract hope from hopelessness. There is no better source of encouragement than God's Word. I encourage you to lean upon these scriptures and others in the Bible to help you find the hope you need to keep going until you see a breakthrough in your life.

Scripture in Conversation with Roger

Romans 7:15, 19–20, NIV

I do not understand what I do. For what I want to do I do not do, but what I hate I do. For what I do is not the good I want to do; no, the evil I do not want to do--this I keep on doing. Now if I do what I do not want to do, it is no longer I who do it, but it is sin living in me that does it.

2 Corinthians 10:3–5, KJV

For though we walk in the flesh, we do not war after the flesh: (For the weapons of our warfare [are] not carnal, but mighty through

God to the pulling down of strong holds;) Casting down imaginations, and every high thing that exalteth itself against the knowledge of God, and bringing into captivity every thought to the obedience of Christ.

Luke 10:19, AMP

I have given you authority to trample on snakes and scorpions and to overcome all the power of the enemy; nothing will harm you.

My Marriage was Falling Apart

1 Corinthians 13:4–7, NIV

Love is patient, love is kind. It does not envy, it does not boast, it is not proud. It is not rude, it is not self-seeking, it is not easily angered, it keeps no record of wrongs. Love does not delight in evil but rejoices with the truth. It always protects, always trusts, always hopes, always perseveres.

Ephesians 6:12, ASV

For our wrestling is not against flesh and blood, but against the principalities, against the powers, against the world-rulers of this darkness, against the spiritual [hosts] of wickedness in the heavenly [places].

John 10:10, ASV

The thief cometh not, but that he may steal, and kill, and destroy: I came that they may have life, and may have [it] abundantly.

Proverbs 3:5–6, NIV
Trust in the LORD with all your heart and lean not on your own understanding; in all your ways acknowledge him, and he will make your paths straight.

Not Knowing My Future

Jeremiah 29:11, NIV
"For I know the plans I have for you," says the LORD. "They are plans for good and not for disaster, to give you a future and a hope."

Isaiah 55:8–12, NIV
"My thoughts are nothing like your thoughts," says the LORD. And my ways are far beyond anything you could imagine. For just as the heavens are higher than the earth, so my ways are higher than your ways and my thoughts higher than your thoughts. The rain and snow come down from the heavens and stay on the ground to water the earth. They cause the grain to grow, producing seed for the farmer and bread for the hungry. It is the same with my word. I send it out, and it always produces fruit. It will accomplish all I want it to, and it will prosper everywhere I send it. You will live in joy and peace. The mountains and hills will burst into song, and the trees of the field will clap their hands!"

Psalm 31:15–24, NIV
My future is in your hands…Let your favor shine on your servant. In your unfailing love, rescue me. Don't let me be disgraced, O LORD, for I call out to you for help. Let the wicked be disgraced; let them lie silent in the grave. Silence their lying lips—those proud and arrogant lips that accuse the godly. How great is the goodness you have

stored up for those who fear you. You lavish it on those who come to you for protection, blessing them before the watching world. You hide them in the shelter of your presence, safe from those who conspire against them. You shelter them in your presence, far from accusing tongues. Praise the LORD, for he has shown me the wonders of his unfailing love. He kept me safe when my city was under attack. In panic I cried out, "I am cut off from the LORD!" But you heard my cry for mercy and answered my call for help. Love the LORD, all you godly ones! For the LORD protects those who are loyal to him…So be strong and courageous, all you who put your hope in the LORD!

Psalm 46:1, 10, NIV
God is our refuge and strength, an ever-present help in trouble. … "Be still, and know that I am God.…"

My Agonizing Dilemma Concerning a Decision on Divorce

Psalm 55:1–2, 4–5, NIV
Listen to my prayer, O God. Do not ignore my cry for help! Please listen and answer me, for I am overwhelmed by my troubles. My heart pounds in my chest. The terror of death assaults me. Fear and trembling overwhelm me, and I can't stop shaking.

Seeking Counsel, Wanting Relief

Psalm 55:6–7, NIV
Oh, that I had wings like a dove; then I would fly away and rest! I would fly far away to the quiet of the wilderness.

Psalm 62:1, NIV
Let all that I am wait quietly before God, for my salvation comes from him.

Psalm 63:2–8, NIV
I have seen you in your sanctuary and gazed upon your power and glory. Your unfailing love is better than life itself; how I praise you! I will praise you as long as I live, lifting up my hands to you in prayer. You satisfy me more than the richest feast. I will praise you with songs of joy. I lie awake thinking of you, meditating on you through the night. Because you are my helper, I sing for joy in the shadow of your wings. I cling to you; your strong right hand holds me securely.

Psalm 84:11, NLT
For the LORD God is our sun and our shield. He gives us grace and glory. The LORD will withhold no good thing from those who do what is right.

Intervention

Ephesians 5:11–14, NIV
Take no part in the worthless deeds of evil and darkness; instead, expose them. It is shameful even to talk about the things that ungodly people do in secret. But their evil intentions will be exposed when the light shines on them, for the light makes everything visible.

My Home, My Refuge

Psalm 127:1–2, NIV
Unless the LORD builds a house, the work of the builders is wasted. Unless the LORD protects a city, guarding it with sentries will do no good. It is useless for you to work so hard from early morning

until late at night, anxiously working for food to eat; for God gives rest to his loved ones.

Psalm 90:1–2, NIV
A PRAYER OF MOSES, THE MAN OF GOD. Lord, through all the generations you have been our home! Before the mountains were born, before you gave birth to the earth and the world, from beginning to end, you are God.

When Feeling Hopeless

Psalm 30:11–12, NIV
You have turned my mourning into joyful dancing. You have taken away my clothes of mourning and clothed me with joy, that I might sing praises to you and not be silent. O LORD my God, I will give you thanks forever!

Right After the Divorce, Trying to Figure Out my Direction

Psalm 25:16–20, NIV
Turn to me and have mercy, for I am alone and in deep distress. My problems go from bad to worse. Oh, save me from them all! Feel my pain and see my trouble. Forgive all my sins. See how many enemies I have and how viciously they hate me! Protect me! Rescue my life from them! Do not let me be disgraced, for in you I take refuge.

Why is Everything Such a Struggle?

Isaiah 54:2–4, NIV
"Enlarge your house; build an addition. Spread out your home, and spare no expense! For you will soon be bursting at the seams. Your descendants will occupy other nations and resettle the ruined cities.

Fear not; you will no longer live in shame. Don't be afraid; there is no more disgrace for you. You will no longer remember the shame of your youth and the sorrows of widowhood."

Zephaniah 3:17–20, NIV

"For the LORD your God is living among you. He is a mighty savior. He will take delight in you with gladness. With his love, he will calm all your fears. He will rejoice over you with joyful songs." I will gather you who mourn for the appointed festivals; you will be disgraced no more. And I will deal severely with all who have oppressed you. I will save the weak and helpless ones; I will bring together those who were chased away. I will give glory and fame to my former exiles, wherever they have been mocked and shamed. On that day I will gather you together and bring you home again. I will give you a good name, a name of distinction, among all the nations of the earth, as I restore your fortunes before their very eyes. I, the LORD, have spoken!"

Lord Vindicate Me!

Psalm 26:1–3, NIV

Declare me innocent, O LORD, for I have acted with integrity; I have trusted in the LORD without wavering. Put me on trial, LORD, and cross-examine me. Test my motives and my heart. For I am always aware of your unfailing love, and I have lived according to your truth.

Help Me to Wait and Believe

Psalm 27:13–14, NIV

Yet I am confident I will see the LORD's goodness while I am here in the land of the living. Wait patiently for the LORD. Be brave and courageous. Yes, wait patiently for the LORD.

Philippians 4:8–9, NIV

Finally, brothers, whatever is true, whatever is noble, whatever is right, whatever is pure, whatever is lovely, whatever is admirable--if anything is excellent or praiseworthy--think about such things. Whatever you have learned or received or heard from me, or seen in me--put it into practice. And the God of peace will be with you.

For My Children and Myself

Psalm 29:11, NIV

The LORD gives his people strength. The LORD blesses them with peace.

Isaiah 54:13, NIV

I will teach all your children, and they will enjoy great peace.

Regarding Insufficiency with Rent Money

Psalm 31:1–3, NIV

O LORD, I have come to you for protection; don't let me be disgraced. Save me, for you do what is right. Turn your ear to listen to me; rescue me quickly. Be my rock of protection, a fortress where I will be safe. You are my rock and my fortress. For the honor of your name, lead me out of this danger.

Committed Myself to the Lord

Psalm 31:5, NIV

I entrust my spirit into your hand. Rescue me, LORD, for you are a faithful God.

My Deepest Feelings about Roger's Drug Use

Psalm 31:7–10, NIV

I will be glad and rejoice in your unfailing love, for you have seen my troubles, and you care about the anguish of my soul. You have not handed me over to my enemies but have set me in a safe place. Have mercy on me, LORD, for I am in distress. Tears blur my eyes. My body and soul are withering away. I am dying from grief; my years are shortened by sadness. Sin has drained my strength; I am wasting away from within.

How Can my Friends Relate?

Psalm 31:11, NIV

I am scorned by all my enemies and despised by my neighbors—even my friends are afraid to come near me. When they see me on the street, they run the other way.

Overwhelming Problems

Psalm 31:12–13, NIV

I am ignored as if I were dead, as if I were a broken pot. I have heard the many rumors about me, and I am surrounded by terror. My enemies conspire against me, plotting to take my life.

Psalm 32:7–8, 10, NIV

For you are my hiding place; you protect me from trouble. You surround me with songs of victory. The LORD says, "I will guide you along the best pathway for your life. I will advise you and watch over you. …but unfailing love surrounds those who trust the LORD.

Psalm 33:4, NLT

For the word of the LORD holds true, and we can trust everything he does.

Psalm 34:15–20, NIV

The eyes of the LORD watch over those who do right; his ears are open to their cries for help. But the LORD turns his face against those who do evil; he will erase their memory from the earth. The LORD hears his people when they call to him for help. He rescues them from all their troubles. The LORD is close to the brokenhearted; he rescues those whose spirits are crushed. The righteous person faces many troubles, but the LORD comes to the rescue each time. For the LORD protects the bones of the righteous; not one of them is broken!

For Me and the Kids

Psalm 34:8–10, NIV

Taste and see that the LORD is good. Oh, the joys of those who take refuge in him! Fear the LORD, you his godly people, for those who fear him will have all they need. …but those who trust in the LORD will lack no good thing.

16905896R00110

Made in the USA
Lexington, KY
16 August 2012